DESIGN GRAPHS FOR BRICK/BLOCK DOUBLE SKIN PANEL WALLS

DESIGN GRAPHS FOR BRICK/BLOCK DOUBLE SKIN PANEL WALLS

C. WILBY

Analyst/Programmer, Highways and Transportation Department, Kent County Council, Maidstone, Kent, UK

APPLIED SCIENCE PUBLISHERS LTD
LONDON

APPLIED SCIENCE PUBLISHERS LTD
RIPPLE ROAD, BARKING, ESSEX, ENGLAND

British Library Cataloguing in Publication Data

Wilby, Christopher Bryan
  Design graphs for brick/block double skin
  panel walls.
  1. Brick walls—Handbooks, manuals, etc.
  2. Wall panels—Handbooks, manuals, etc.
  I. Title
  693'.4   TH2243

  ISBN 0-85334-945-2

Printed in Great Britain by Galliard (Printers) Ltd, Great Yarmouth

The type of wall considered has always been a very satisfactory construction
for thermal, acoustic and damp insulation and hence enjoys continuing
popularity and may increase its popularity because of increasing interest
in energy saving.

This type of wall has traditionally been designed by the experience of an
engineer making an initial guess of the wall type suitable and then pursuing
a check of his assumption. This process tends to either give stronger walls
than necessary because of the limited time available to optimize on a
solution, or waste valuable time if a weaker wall had been chosen initially
and several extra guesses had to be investigated.

Now with the use of the graphs provided in this book an optimum assessment of a suitable wall can be chosen directly from the graphs. Hence
architects can obtain instant decisions on what type of wall to use without referral to their engineers.

The design process begins with an assessment of the wind speed and hence
design wind load for the location where a panel wall is required. A wall
type is then chosen and analysed. This process is long and repetitive
when several tries for the optimum type are made. Therefore the purpose
of the graphs presented is to enable the designer to choose rapidly an
optimum wall type for the panel required and also to adjust the design at
an early stage to suit a wall which may be required.

The graphs show wind load on the vertical axis against length on the
horizontal axis for specific restraint conditions and a shape factor
relating length to height. Thus a panel size with set restraint conditions
and of known length which has to withstand a specific wind loading can have
a wall type chosen for it instantly by using the graphs.

The graphs were worked out and drawn by a computer program, the data consisting of the most commonly used brick and mortar types used with safety factors for normal construction. Design is in accordance with the code of practice for unreinforced masonry BS.5628:Pt. 1:1978.

The graphs presented are based on wind load rather than wind speed and deal with wind loads up to 2.5 kN/m^2. In certain circumstances these may be related to wind speed up to and in excess of 63 m/s using the Code of Practice for Loading CP.3, Chap. V, Pt. 2, Wind Loads, of the British Standards Institution.

The range of wind speeds is in excess of those used for design in the UK and is adequate for many countries worldwide. Some of these countries will use the British code, and some countries will have no guidance in their code on this matter and will appreciate using the British code for the particular designs. A Danish consultant at a recent conference in Athens said 'Whatever happens to you British, you have given the world your language and your British Standards and Codes of Practice' and went on to say that he (a Dane) used British codes for his designs in many countries both with and without former British connections.

In the fairly unlikely event of a design needing to be made in some locality with higher wind speeds than given by the graphs, extrapolation presents no particular difficulty as can be appreciated by studying the curves (i.e. their asymptotic nature at higher wind loads).

The book should be of use to practising Structural Engineers and Architects and to undergraduate and postgraduate Structural Engineering and Architectural Students in their design classes.

The graphs in this book are particularly valuable for checking of designs for approval by the various local authorities.

Section 1.4 has been produced to help non-British engineers both using and not using various British codes.

All graphs and tables in this book have been prepared with every care, but are not intended to be used to take away from a consultant the responsibility for his own designs. He may use the graphs and tables for speed of design or as a check but should assure himself that his design is sound, for example by approximate independent checks plus his experience or by accurate independent checks. The graphs produced have been thoroughly checked by a practising engineer, namely Mr R. Marshall, B.Sc., C.Eng., M.I.C.E., M.I.Struct.E. Many thanks are due to Mr Marshall for his perseverance, guidance and useful advice concerning the presentation of the graphs for ease of use by practising engineers.

An example at random has been produced by normal non-computer methods in Section 2.1 and it can be seen that this is in agreement with the design graphs; the comparable solution using the design graphs being given in Section 3.2.

TO

SIÂN

CONTENTS

Chapter 5   Program Information

NOMENCLATURE

Most symbols are explained when required in the book. The remaining
symbols are as follows:

α bending moment coefficient for laterally loaded panels

h   height of wall

L   length of panel

W_k characteristic wind load

Chapter 1

INTRODUCTION TO PANEL WALLS

1.1 INTRODUCTION

A brick/block wall has traditionally been designed as either cantilevering from its footing (as either a free or propped cantilever) or horizontally spanning between two piers or stiffening walls. These methods are perfectly acceptable but for the majority of cases considerably underestimate the strength of a panel. A wall is considered to be a panel when its shape factor (height divided by length, both being measured to supports or free edges) is within the range 0.3 to 1.75. A wall with a shape factor below 0.3 will tend to act as cantilevering or spanning vertically, whilst shape factors above 1.75 give walls tending to span horizontally.

The code of practice CP.111[1] gave bending moment coefficients for walls cantilevering (freely or propped) and horizontally spanning, leaving the designer to choose the most suitable for his purposes. There was no guidance on the design of panel type walls.

For some time, codes of practice (thus to some extent researchers) and designers have treated brickwork as generally analogous to concrete in its properties (the bricks merely being large pieces of aggregate) and having different strengths in mutually perpendicular directions. Table 7 of the code of practice BS.5628[2] gives bending moment coefficients for fixed edge moments and span moments. This particular code is different from CP.111[1] which it is intended to replace in the following respects:

(a) It uses limit state philosophy in accordance with recent practice with other codes. This philosophy was agreed generally with Europe and is now finding its way into new British and American codes. For example, the first seem to have been the codes on structural concrete in the U.K. and U.S.A.

I

(b) It excludes plain concrete walls which are now dealt with by CP.110.[3]

(c) It gives guidance on the design of walls to resist lateral loading, because of 'the widespread demand for guidance on the design of walls to resist lateral loading'.

This latter point is the subject of this present book. With regard to the design of walls to resist lateral loads BS.5628[2] has been based on a combination of theoretical propositions, experimental research and practical experience. It was suggested[4,5] that there were a number of ways in which bending moments could be obtained for designing panel walls, viz.:

(1) elastic plate methods, after Timoshenko,[6]

(2) yield line theory, after Johansen,[7]

(3) finite elements,

(4) empirical.

In ref. 5 several methods of design were compared with experimental results and 'an interim one based on yield-line theory is favoured'. A semi-empirical approach was also examined. The possibility of arching action was considered but no allowance made for it so that it can be considered as providing a hidden reserve of safety.

Yield line theory was devised[7] for reinforced concrete slabs. It assumes that the bending moment at the point of initial maximum bending moment on a 'yield line' reaches a yield value and stays constant whilst other portions of that line reach that yield value. A pattern of yield lines develops with constant moment along each line to give a collapse mechanism. A brick wall could not be expected to hold a constant moment at one point whilst further loading was being resisted by other portions of the wall, as there is no steel reinforcement to yield, and the brickwork would fail as soon as its resistance moment was reached.

Haseltine et al.[5] make the point that applying yield line theory to brickwork has one considerable advantage in that it is possible to use in the calculations different strengths in two orthogonal directions, enabling bending moment coefficients to be obtained for panels using the actual ratio of strengths, so that each direction will contribute equally. The calculations can also allow for any bending resistance over a support as a ratio of the available resistance to the strength of the brickwork in the relevant direction.

As stated in (a) above, the code of practice uses limit state design philosophy. That is the structure is designed to fail with factors of

safety applied to the loading on, and to the strengths of the materials in
the structure. For the limit state of serviceability deflection is not
critical, but cracking is critical. The ultimate limit state (i.e. collapse
of the masonry) is the over-riding factor in design but cracking has also to
be considered. It is known that the limit states of cracking and collapse
occur almost simultaneously. Therefore only the collapse limit state need
be considered.

The limit state of deflection is not critical because masonry walls are
basically weak in bending, because of their relatively low tensile strength,
and therefore the large sections required to withstand bending moments
ensure walls which are quite stiff and not troubled by deflection due to
bending.

To ensure that the ultimate limit state is not reached, the code[2] gives
partial safety factors (see Clause 22 and Table 4 in the Code) which are
applied to loads and to material strengths. In the case of laterally loaded
wall panels the code gives a partial safety factor of 1.2 to be applied to
wind loading. Partial safety factors for material strength depend upon
construction control and manufacturing control. There are two categories
of construction control.[2] These are 'special' and 'normal'. For 'special'
to be selected, there should be adequate supervision of work in accordance
with Clause 4.14 in CP.121,[8] and 'normal' is selected when there is not
this degree of supervision. Manufacturing control also falls into two
categories. These are 'special' and 'normal'. The special category is
chosen when it is guaranteed that not more than $2\frac{1}{2}\%$ of bricks fall below
the specified compressive strength. Normal control is when this condition
cannot be guaranteed. In practice the 'normal' category is usually applied
for both construction and manufacturing control hence giving a material
strength factor of 3.5 (see Table 4 of ref. 2). If any other factor is
chosen when using the graphs, which are all for the factor of 3.5, the wind
loading or length obtained needs to be multiplied by the ratio of 3.5
divided by the factor chosen. Material strengths are defined as characteristic strengths,[2] viz. characteristic compressive strength of masonry,
characteristic flexural strength of masonry and characteristic shear strength
of masonry. The experimental determination of these values is closely
defined in Appendix A of ref. 2.

The ratio of limiting vertical flexural strength to limiting horizontal
flexural strength of a panel is referred to as the 'orthogonal stress ratio'
(μ). This is used in Table 7[2] to obtain bending moment coefficients which

are then applied to the different skins of a panel. The failure load is
the same whether the bending strengths are considered for horizontal or
vertical spans due to the moment coefficient vertically being related to
the moment coefficient horizontally by the ratio μ which is also the ratio
between flexural vertical and horizontal strengths. Thus only failure in
the horizontal direction needs to be calculated.[9] When in addition to the
above bending moments, vertical load is carried by the wall, this dead load
requires[2] a partial safety factor of 0.9. It increases the vertical flexural
strength (by in effect prestressing the section) and hence the orthogonal
ratio μ. This reduces the value of the moment coefficients with the effect
that greater lateral loads can be carried by the panel. This effect thus
adds to the strength of the wall available to resist lateral loading, but
it is only significant when large vertical loads are applied. Therefore
the graphs do not take account of vertical loading. It would be practically
impossible to include vertical loading on the graphs because of the infinite
number of combinations of vertical and horizontal loading which could occur.
The graphs thus guarantee the strength of panels with or without vertical
loading; this vertical loading serving to increase the overall factor of
safety of such panels.

The strength of a wall depends upon the following factors:

(1) flexural strength in each of the two orthogonal directions,

(2) shear strength of the brickwork,

(3) thickness of the wall,

(4) size and shape of wall,

(5) quality of workmanship.

Wind loads are the main criteria for the design of panels. The strength
of brickwork/blockwork is high in compression and relatively very low in
tension. Lateral loads produce bending moments promoting flexural tension
in a wall. Walls have, over the years, become more slender as more information about design has become available. Also, recently, because of
failures and further research, the wind pressures for which walls are
designed[10] have increased enormously. Thus wind load has become the pre-
dominant factor in panel wall design. In most cases if a wall is satisfied
for lateral loading, it will inevitably be satisfactory for vertical loading,
either on its own or in addition to the lateral loading.

Walls can be sub-divided into two types, 'external' and 'internal'.
External walls are designed to resist lateral loading as well as vertical

loads whilst internal are only needed for vertical loading (e.g. partition walls inside building structures). The set of graphs presented are intended to be used when designing external walls (namely panels). Most external walls are double skin in order to satisfy the building regulations and provide enough insulation to the occupants. Panel walls are invariably used throughout. A panel wall is defined by its shape. The shape, height divided by length, must not be greater than 1.75 or less than 0.3. When the shape is greater than 1.75 the wall is designed to span horizontally like a simple beam and when the shape is less than 0.3 then walls are designed to span vertically like a simple cantilever. Brickwork, and even more so blockwork, are materials susceptible to temperature changes and hence expand or contract with changes in temperature. Therefore contraction joints are often required (usually at about 12 m centres) which will affect the restraint of a panel. That is, an edge loses its continuity and changes from a fixed support to simply supported or free depending upon other restraint from behind.

The design graphs in this book can therefore be used for quickly designing, or checking the adequacy of design, of brick/block (masonry) panel walls. The design graphs ensure the adequacy of panel walls using the latest reliable information, expressed in terms of modern limit state philosophy, for the resistance of walls to modern high wind pressures (resulting from the study of collapses and modern research); as embodied in the latest British Codes of Practice.[2,10] By modern high wind pressures is meant the modern realization, as a result of collapses having occurred, that the wind pressures previously used in design were very significantly too low.

1.2 AIM OF BOOK

The new code for designing unreinforced brickwork or blockwork walls[2] is very different from the previous code.[1] It is more complex and designs are more difficult and take considerably more time to produce. It also gives a realistic design method for panel walls; the previous code not considering panel walls.

This book enables walls to be designed rapidly by using the design graphs. This means that an architect or engineer decides that he requires a panel wall of a certain area. He then calculates the wind loading.[10] By using the design graphs of this book he can quickly find whether various types of walls are adequate in accordance with the new code.[2] Thus the architect can decide immediately, at an early design stage, upon the structurally correct wall to use. This saves time when he is later assisted by the structural engineer in that no alteration is required and if the engineer also uses the design graphs he too saves considerable time making his decisions.

At the early design stage the architect decides upon the layout and he will have the opportunity of varying this to give more efficient designs of wall panels, leading to considerable economies, because for example all the walls of a building could be affected. At present and in the past, architects have usually chosen the layout and assessed the wall design from past experience. When this is later checked by the structural engineer it may well be safe, but may be capable of slight, or occasionally considerable, economies by revising the layout, but it is often too late at that stage. Those architects who could fairly quickly design walls using the previous code will not now be able to make these speedy designs using the new code without the use of the design graphs in this book.

Thus the design graphs in this book will enable an architectural office to make considerable economies in the design of walls. They will also enable structural engineers to rapidly check the designs of others and to produce their own designs. The design graphs should therefore be most useful to those concerned with designing and/or checking the designs of brick/block walls.

1.3   USE OF DESIGN GRAPHS

Further to Section 1.2 the use of the design graphs for checking a given panel wall is as follows:

Step 1: Determine using ref. 10 (or the code of the country concerned) the wind speed to be used and the consequent resultant pressure the wall is required to withstand.

Step 2: Assess the type of fixity (i.e. whether free, simply supported or fixed) of each edge.

Step 3: Select the appropriate restraint case, see Section 4.1.

Step 4: Calculate the shape factor for the panel thus:

$$\text{shape factor} = \frac{\text{height of panel } (LY)}{\text{length of panel } (LX)}$$

Step 5: Choose the relevant graph from the information obtained in steps 3 and 4.

<u>Step 6</u>: Determine the wind load (which the wall can safely withstand) on the vertical axis from the length of the panel (on the horizontal axis) and the wall type curve (see Section 4.1).

<u>Step 7</u>: If the wind load obtained from step 6 is greater than that given by step 1 then the wall is satisfactory for strength.

In designing a building the heights between floors will be decided by planning considerations and the structural floor thickness, and the structural floor system will be decided from planning considerations, layout of columns etc. and structural possibilities. These considerations will have decided the spacing of the external columns and the distances between floors, that is the geometry of the panels. To use the design graphs for designing a wall the procedure is as follows:

<u>Steps 1 to 5</u>: as previously.

<u>Step 6</u>: From the wind load on the vertical axis and from the length on the horizontal axis a point on the graph can be determined. The curves (representing wall types) which are below this point do not fulfil strength requirements. Any curves above will be adequate to use and hence a choice is made from these.

1.4   <u>USE OF DESIGN GRAPHS INTERNATIONALLY</u>

A Danish consultant recently said 'whatever happens to you British, you have given the world your language and your British Standards and Codes of Practice'. It is impossible to write one book in a multi language and to satisfy the practices of all countries. However, the English language with the help of the U.S.A. and northern Europeans, who find English easier to speak and learn than for example French, Spanish, Russian or Chinese, has become well ahead of all other languages in international technology. Many countries internationally allow the use of British Standards and Codes of Practice.

Hence the design graphs in this book are useful to architects and engineers in a great many countries. The graphs and all the work in the book use S.I. units. These were recommended by an international committee formed to rationalise the use of the metric system as it had, for example become rather untidy in its use in Europe (e.g. drawings in some countries would use metres and millimetres whereas in other countries they would use metres and centimetres). It was a considerable task for the U.K. to convert to the use of S.I. units. The U.S.A. and Canada have of recent years been making a change to S.I. units in technological papers. For the benefit of those who have not yet converted to S.I. units it is useful, so that they can be sure to use the design graphs correctly and to give undoubted definition to the design graphs to give the following conversion units:

British Imperial	U.S.A.	Metric	S.I. unit
1 ton	1 long ton	1016.0 kg	9.964 kN
2000 lb	1 short ton	907.1 kg	8.896 kN
0.9843 ton	0.9843 long tons	1 tonne (1000 kg)	9.807 kN
1 lb	1 lb	0.4536 kg	4.448 N
1000 lb	1 kip.	453.6 kg	4.448 kN
1 inch	1 inch	2.54 cm	25.4 mm
1 foot	1 foot	30.48 cm	0.3048 m
1000 lb in	1 kip in	1152 kg cm	0.1130 kN m
1000 lb/in	1 kip/in	178.6 kg/cm	175.1 kN/m
1 lb/in^2	1 p.s.i.	0.070309 kg/cm^2	6.895 kN/m^2
1000 lb/in^2	1 kip/in^2 (1000 p.s.i.)	70.309 kg/cm^2	6.895 N/mm^2
1 lb/ft^2	1 lb/ft^2	4.882 kg/m^2	0.04788 kN/m^2
1 ton/ft^2	1 long ton/ft^2	10.940 kg/m^2	107.3 kN/m^2
1 lb/ft	1 lb/ft	1.488 kg/m	0.01459 kN/m
1 ton/ft	1 long ton/ft	3333 kg/m	32.69 kN/m
1 lb/ft^3	1 lb/ft^3	16.02 kg/m^3	0.15707 kN/m^3

(N.B. the terms force and mass have not been used above, and gravity = 9.807 m/s^2)

Those workers in countries which use non-British codes for wind pressure can use the design graphs of this book. They just determine the lateral wind pressure on the wall in N/mm^2 units from the code of practice which they favour and then make use of the design graphs as described in Section 1.3. This would give the wall the security afforded by the latest British code of practice. The procedure for designing a panel wall is thus as follows:

Step 1: Determine the wind pressure which the panel has to be designed to carry.

Step 2: Assess the type of fixity (i.e. whether free, simply supported or fixed) of each edge.

Step 3: Select the appropriate restraint case, see Section 4.1 (Fig. 4.1 and Table 4.1).

Step 4: Calculate the shape factor for the panel thus:

$$\text{shape factor} = \frac{\text{height of panel (LY)}}{\text{length of panel (LX)}}$$

Step 5: Choose the relevant graph from the information obtained in Steps 3 and 4.

Step 6: From the wind pressure on the vertical axis and from the length on the horizontal axis a point on the graph can be determined. Any curves above (and to the right of) this point give the wall types which can be used. The curves should be counted from left to right or bottom to top. The number obtained in this way gives the number of the wall type. Details of these wall types are given in Section 4.1 (Fig. 4.2). The specifications of the bricks, blocks and mortar for these wall types are given in Section 3.1. If an existing wall has to be checked for strength, then the procedure to follow is as follows:

Steps 1 to 5: as previously.

Step 6: Decide for the brick or blocks and mortar and the wall geometry, using Section 4.1 (Fig. 4.2) for geometry and Section 3.1 (Table 3.1) for brick, block and mortar specification, the wall type number. On the design curve read the span on the horizontal axis, then take a vertical line to hit the curve representing the wall type number (these are counted from bottom to top which is the same as from left to right). From this point take a horizontal line to read the wind pressure which the wall can resist on the vertical axis. This wind pressure will then be related to the locality with methods approved by the country or state concerned.

Chapter 2

THEORY AND ANALYSIS

2.1 EXAMPLE OF DESIGN OF A TYPICAL BRICK/BLOCK PANEL

The Table and Clause numbers and Cases given in this example are from ref.
2. This example was produced in the traditional way in accordance with the
British Code of Practice to show those who use the code that the design
graphs, see Section 3.2, can be used instead. Internationally when the
British Code is not specified, the design curves can still be used as
described in Section 1.4.

2.1.1 Dynamic load

The lateral load from wind forces varies greatly on a masonry panel,
depending upon the location and configuration of the building in which it
is constructed. When designing a particular panel the wind loading on the
panel should be calculated according to ref. 10 but for the purposes of
this example the dynamic loading will be assumed to be 710 N/m^2.

2.1.2 Assumed wall panel data:

Size of panel:	6 m long x 3 m high
Fixity:	sides fixed, base and top pinned; (Case G, Table 9)
Brick outer leaf:	clay bricks 102.5 mm thick; 10% water absorption
Block inner leaf:	concrete blocks 100 mm thick, compressive strength 3.5 N/mm^2
Mortar:	1:1:5, cement:lime:sand

2.1.3 <u>Design data:</u>

Characteristic flexural strength = f_{kx} N/mm^2 (Table 3)

(Vertical failure)   (Horizontal failure)

For brickwork: f_{kx} = 0.4 N/mm^2 and f_{kx} = 1.1 N/mm^2

For blockwork: f_{kx} = 0.25 N/mm^2 and f_{kx} = 0.45 N/mm^2

Partial safety factor loads, γ_f = 1.2   (Clause 22)

Partial safety factor for materials γ_m = 3.5   (Clause 27.3)

Orthogonal strength ratio = μ

For brickwork: $\mu = \dfrac{0.4}{1.1} = 0.364$

For blockwork: $\mu = \dfrac{0.25}{0.45} = 0.556$ (Clause 36.4.2)

2.1.4 <u>Design of panel</u>

Design moment of resistance = $\dfrac{f_{kx} \, Z}{\gamma_m} = M_r$ (Clause 36.4.3)

where Z = section modulus

For brickwork: $Z = \dfrac{1000 \times 102.5^2}{6} = 1.751 \times 10^6$ mm^3

For blockwork: $Z = \dfrac{1000 \times 100^2}{6} = 1.667 \times 10^6$ mm^3

Therefore, M_r brickwork $= \dfrac{1.1 \times 1.75 \times 10^6}{3.5} = 0.55 \times 10^6$ N mm

$= 0.55$ kN m

M_r blockwork $= \dfrac{0.45 \times 1.67 \times 10^6}{3.5} = 0.215 \times 10^6$ N mm

$= 0.215$ kN m

where M_r = design moment of resistance

The applied load is shared by the two leaves in proportion to their design moments of resistance (Clause 36.4.5)

Therefore, Load to be carried by brickwork $= \dfrac{0.55}{(0.55 + 0.215)} \times 0.710$

$= 0.511$ kN/m^2

Load to be carried by blockwork $= \dfrac{0.215}{(0.55 + 0.215)} \times 0.710$

$= 0.200$ kN/m^2

Referring to Table 9 case G h/L = 0.5

For brickwork: μ = 0.364 ; therefore, α = 0.0243

For blockwork: μ = 0.556 ; therefore, α = 0.0199

Design moment = $\alpha \, W_k \, \gamma_f \, L^2$ (Clause 36.4.2)

For brickwork, M_u = 0.0243 × 0.511 × 1.2 × 6^2 = 0.536 kN m

For blockwork, M_u = 0.0199 × 0.200 × 1.2 × 6^2 = 0.171 kN m

These two values are not greater than their respective design moments
of resistance (determined above) of 0.55 and 0.215 kN m and therefore
the panel is satisfactory.

2.2   VARIATIONS TO IDEAL CONDITIONS OF LOADING (LINE LOADS, POINT LOADS, DAMP-PROOF COURSES)

2.2.1 Line loads

This type of loading generally occurs when an opening is incorporated into
a panel. A window or door would be most likely to cause such an opening to
be formed. The opening gives the panel a new irregular shape not covered by
the graphs in this book.

In the case of small framed openings it is expected that the wall will
have no reduction in strength if the frame is of sufficient strength and
tightly fitted. Therefore the presence of such openings will not affect
design by the graphs.

Larger openings deem it necessary to split the wall into rectangular
shapes around each opening. For example in Fig. 2.1 panel (a) contains a
window. This panel can be split into the panels shown in Fig. 2.1 (b) and
(c). The window frame mainly transmits the loading on the window in the
direction of the shorter span, i.e. the top and bottom supports of the window
frame so that the panel shown in Fig. 2.1 (b) can be assumed to have a free
edge at the opening. The panel shown in Fig. 2.1 (b) is also assumed to be
fixed where it has been detached from the panel shown in Fig. 2.1 (c). Thus
the panel shown in Fig. 2.1 (b) transmits loading to the top of the panel
shown in Fig. 2.1 (c). The amount of this load transmitted is assumed to
be half of the wind load on the panel shown in Fig. 2.1 (b). This latter
panel is simply supported on two other edges so that this is a simplification,
and in fact less than half of its load will be transmitted to the top edge of
the panel shown in Fig. 2.1 (c). The true amount of load transmitted is
indeterminate, and for simplicity half is assumed. The same applies with
the window frame opening. Thus half of the loading on the panel shown in
Fig. 2.1 (b) and the window is assumed to act on a horizontal strip at the
top of the wall. The width of this strip is indeterminate but 300 mm is a
reasonable assumption.[9] This strip can then be analysed as spanning horizontally. The panel shown in Fig. 2.1 (d) can be designed using the graphs
and having the restraint shown in this figure.

Figure 2.2 shows a panel with an opening of height large relative to its

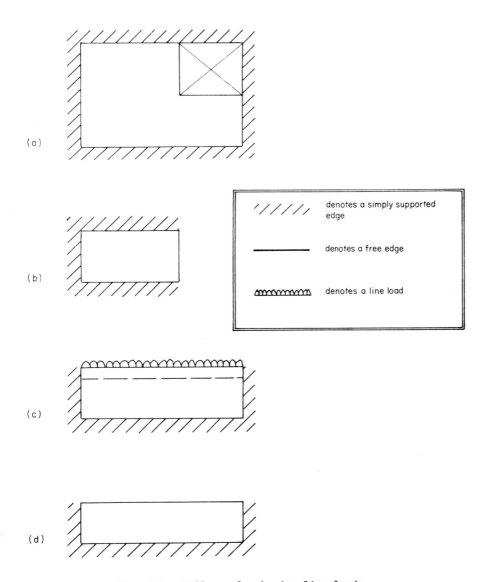

Fig. 2.1. Wall panels showing line loads.

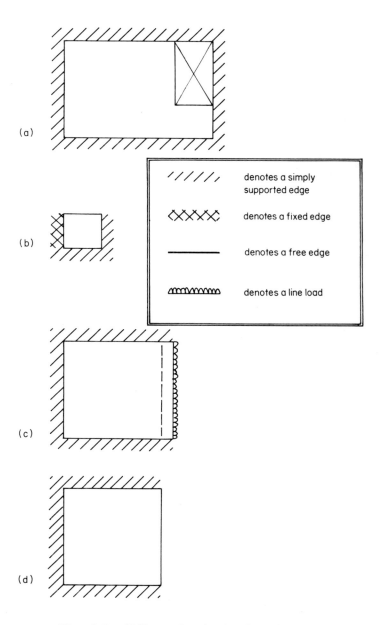

Fig. 2.2.   Wall panels showing line loads.

length. Such a panel would be split into sub-panels differently to the
panel in Fig. 2.1. The opening is assumed to span horizontally thus creating
a line load on the adjacent panel shown in Fig. 2.2 (c). Also the sub-panel
shown in Fig. 2.2 (b) gives a similar effect and its restraint next to the
opening is considered free. The edge of the sub-panel (Fig. 2.2 (b)) adjacent
to the sub-panel shown in Fig. 2.2 (c) is considered as fixed. Thus a line
load is produced and a strip (assumed as 300 mm in width as before) carries
this load in addition to wind loading on the strip itself. This strip is
then designed as a simple beam in the vertical direction. The remaining
part of the panel shown in Fig. 2.2 (d) has a free edge adjacent to the
strip just considered and can be designed using the graphs, but if the strip
is satisfactory then the rest of the panel shown in Fig. 2.2 (d) will be
satisfactory as it can be considered as consisting of a whole series of
strips which have less load on them, but with the same support conditions.
Also the panel shown in Fig. 2.2 (b) will be satisfactory as it has much
smaller spans. It must be noted however that the strength of brickwork/
blockwork in the horizontal direction is greater than the brickwork/block-
work strength in the vertical direction. Therefore in the case of a panel
with an opening with height large relative to width it may be more satisfactory to assume the line load lies horizontally as in Fig. 2.1 depending
upon the horizontal length of the strip carrying the line load. Also it
could be true in Fig. 2.1 that the strip could be taken vertically to give
a better result depending on the span.

When a clerestory window is incorporated in a panel, the window sill may
be designed to span horizontally and thus not impose a line loading on the
panel below. In this case the top of the panel will be assumed free in
its analysis unless the sill beam has been designed to carry extra load from
the panel and then a simply supported or fixed restraint can be assumed. A
panel with a full height opening adjacent to it may be designed as a smaller
panel with a free edge at the opening, providing that the framed opening can
span vertically itself. If the opening cannot span itself then a line load
is carried by the wall in the vertical direction as shown in Fig. 2.2 (c).

2.2.2 <u>Point loads</u>

Wall panels, laterally loaded by wind pressure, are not designed to take
point loads acting laterally. Point loads may however be supported at the
top, or anywhere else on a panel, acting vertically downwards and hence
producing vertical stresses. These act against flexural tensile stresses

produced from the effect of lateral loads. Hence the panel becomes
stronger against lateral loads. Thus the design graphs of this book can
be used in these cases. Naturally for such walls the bearing strength of
the brickwork/blockwork must be adequate under the action of the point
loads and therefore must be checked for adequacy.

2.2.3 Damp-proof courses

A damp-proof course (d.p.c.) invariably has to be inserted at the base of
walls serving to protect occupants from the environment. Damp-proof courses
are of varying types and reference to manufacturers has to be made to obtain
their shearing strengths. Although in general the purpose of a d.p.c. is
not for its strength but for its impermeable qualities important to provide
comfort in buildings and to allow the use of attractive facia bricks, say
with rustic facings above the d.p.c. which do not need to be of a very dense
variety to resist frost action. On this latter point many bricks, with for
example attractive rustic finishes, if they were used say just below the
d.p.c. would become sufficiently saturated for their rustic faces to spall
off due to frost action in the U.K. When a d.p.c. is used it is usually
in the form of a bitumen membrane but can be made of slates or more
expensive high quality engineering bricks.[12] For further information on
d.p.c. types refer to refs. 13 and 14.

When a membrane is inserted at the base of a wall then the restraint will
act as fixed by virtue of the shear strength of the membrane. The shear
strength is enhanced by the self weight of the wall. The fixity remains
until the shear strength of the d.p.c. is exceeded. It is debatable
whether or not a fixed base or pinned base should be assumed and this
obviously depends upon the shear strength of the d.p.c. and upon the self
weight of the wall. In high walls, the base could be assumed to be fixed;
and for low height walls pinned. Thus between low and high rise walls an
approximation between fixed and pinned could be used. But in any type,
if the shear resistance is equivalent to that of the brickwork and mortar,
and the self weight sufficient to eliminate flexural tensile stresses,
then a fixed restraint can be assumed. When engineering bricks are used
as a d.p.c. then there is no doubt involved in making the assumption of
fixity. Results of tests have shown that the inclusion of a d.p.c. membrane
does not significantly affect the failure loads of walls even though the
failure pattern is quite different[15] (see Fig. 2.3). Hence the graphs are
valid in cases using a d.p.c. although some engineering judgement may be
required.

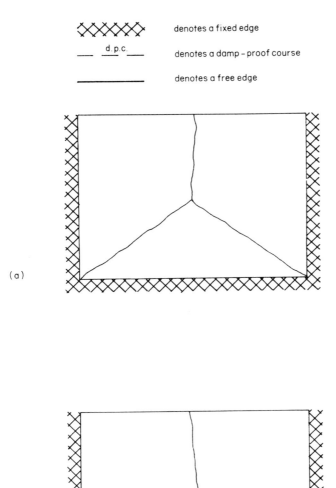

Fig. 2.3. Typical failure patterns for panels (a) with
and (b) without a damp-proof course.

Chapter 3

INTRODUCTION TO DESIGN GRAPHS

3.1   SCOPE OF DESIGN GRAPHS

The design graphs are intended to replace a detailed design of a wall
where each individual panel requires a full calculation as given in Section
2.1.   The designer is however required to obtain the wind pressure on the
panel using whichever code or method he deems appropriate. The British
code[10] gives considerable guidance on this matter.   The designer is also
required to choose the most relevant restraint case (see Fig. 4.1) for the
panel from its particular disposition in the building.   There is plenty of
guidance on this matter in books and codes of practice.   Any previous
education or experience in building construction possessed by the designer
will probably also help with his guidance in this matter.   If the designer
is in doubt about the restraining effects of a certain building construction
he can rapidly assess several possibilities using the graphs of this book and
perhaps take the worst or a compromise with nearly the worst condition.   The
designer will find that the design graphs are useful in quickly determining
the likely construction of a panel when considering alternative solutions at
an early design stage.

The graphs deal with wind loadings up to 2.5 kN/m^2 and panel lengths up
to 10 m for nine different wall constructions.   For the graphs the brickwork
and blockwork characteristics[2] are chosen to be those most commonly used in
practice, and are tabulated in Table 3.1.

3.2   EXAMPLE USING GRAPHS

To illustrate the use of the graphs the example given in Section 2.1 will
be considered.

Characteristics of mortars, bricks and blocks used in the graphs

Item	Description	Reference to B.S. 5628[2]
Mortar	Cement : Lime : Sand Designation 1 :0 to $\frac{1}{4}$: 3 (i) * 1 : $\frac{1}{2}$:4 to $4\frac{1}{2}$ (ii) 1 : 1 :5 to 6 (iii) Masonry cement : sand Designation 1 :$2\frac{1}{2}$ to $3\frac{1}{2}$ (ii) 1 :4 to 5 (iii) Cement : Sand with plasticizer Designation 1 : 3 to 4 (ii) 1 : 5 to 6 (iii)	Table 1
Bricks	Clay bricks having water absorption between 7% and 12% for mortar types (ii) and (iii) Strengths flexural strength parallel to bed joints = 0.4 N/mm^2 flexural strength perpendicular to bed joints = 1.1 N/mm^2	Table 3
Blocks	Concrete blocks of compressive strength for mortar types (i)*, (ii) and (iii) = 3.5 N/mm^2 Strengths flexural strength parallel to bed joints = 0.25 N/mm^2 flexural strength perpendicular to bed joints = 0.45 N/mm^2	Table 3
Factors	Partial safety factor for material strength = 3.5 Partial safety factor for design loads = 1.2	Table 4 Clause 22

Table 3.1

*This mortar type is permitted for blockwork but should not be used for low strength blocks (i.e. less than 3.5 N/mm^2) because then the mortar strength exceeds that of the blockwork and hence serious rupture of the blockwork can easily be caused.

The wind loading is calculated as before and again will be taken as 0.71 kN/m^2. The following data is the same as in Section 2.1:

Panel length = 6 m

Shape factor = 0.5 (see Section 4.1)

Restraint case = G (see Fig. 4.1)

The panel length is read on the horizontal axis and the wind load on the vertical axis of the design graph. The point relevant to these two values is plotted(on the relevant design graph which is reproduced in this Section for the benefit of the reader) and the curve for any wall type above and to the right of this point represents a satisfactory wall type; conversely, any curve below and to the left represents an unsatisfactory wall type. It can be seen on the design graph that when plotting 6 m for panel length and 0.71 kN/m^2 for wind load that the first curve above and to the right is for wall type 3. This means that the minimum strength of construction which is satisfactory is as follows:

Wall type 3 - see Fig. 4.2

Mortar, bricks and blocks - can be as given in
Table 3.1. In this particular example (see Section 2.1)
the materials used were: clay bricks with 10% water
absorption, blocks of 3.5 N/mm^2 compressive strength,
and mortar of 1:1:5 cement:lime:sand (i.e. designated
(iii) in Table 3.1).

On the design graph reproduced here the curves are numbered with wall types. These numbers are always in the same sequence and start from the left-hand side with number 1, thus they are not shown on the graphs reproduced later in the book. The sequence still applies even when there are less than nine curves.

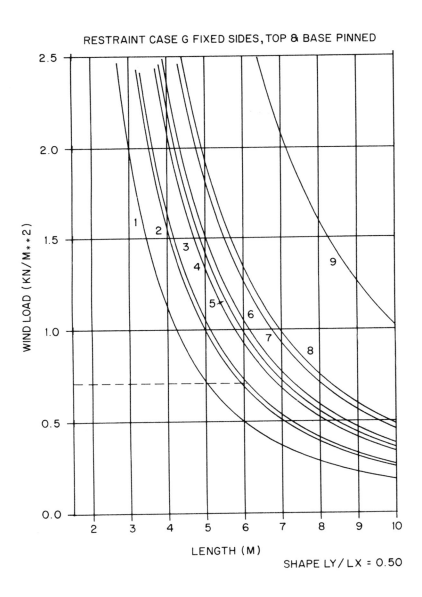

Design Graph

Chapter 4

DESIGN GRAPHS

4.1 NOTES ON DESIGN GRAPHS

Each design graph has an abbreviated title indicating the restraint case
for the panel. There are twelve different restraint cases, Cases A to L
inclusive, in total and these are listed in Table 4.1 and shown diagram-
matically in Fig. 4.1. For each restraint case there are seven different
shape factors which are printed at the lower right hand side of each design
graph. The shape factor, LY/LX, is the ratio of the height of panel, LY,
to the length of the panel, LX; thus defining the panel shape. Hence as
there are some seven different shape factors, viz. 0.30, 0.5, 0.75, 1.00,
1.25, 1.50 and 1.75, for each restraint case, and twelve restraint cases,
there is a total of seven multiplied by twelve design graphs, i.e. a total
of 84 design graphs.

The WIND LOAD, dynamic and pressure,[2] is shown on the vertical axis of
the graph and is given in kilonewtons per square metre. Panel LENGTH is
shown on the horizontal axis and is given in units of metres.

The curves shown on the graphs refer to various wall types. There are
nine different wall types as illustrated in Fig. 4.2. Hence nine curves
are generally shown on each graph. Less than nine curves are shown on some;
this is because the stronger wall types will carry greater load than the
maximum value on the graph. All the wall types given on the design graphs
are double skin walls. The strength of each one is independent of the
direction of the wind, i.e. whether it impinges on one side or the other.

If one wishes to determine the strength of a single skin of brickwork,
then values of wind load given from the curve on any design graph for wall
type 6 should be halved. Similarly if the strength of a single skin of
blockwork is needed then the values from the curve for wall type 1 should

RESTRAINT CASE	ABBREVIATED TITLE (as shown on graphs)	FULL DESCRIPTION
A	Pinned base & sides	The panel base and sides are simply supported and the top is free.
B	Sides fixed & pinned, base pinned	The base and one side are simply supported. The other side is fixed and the top is free.
C	Sides fixed, base pinned	Both sides are fixed and the base is simply supported. The top is free.
D	Fixed sides & base	Both sides and the base are fixed. The top is free.
E	All sides pinned	All the panel edges are simply supported.
F	Side fixed, other edges pinned	One side is fixed and the other three edges are simply supported.
G	Fixed sides, top & base pinned	Both sides are fixed and the top and base are simply supported.
H	Top & sides fixed, base pinned	Both sides and the top are fixed. The base is simply supported.
I	All sides fixed	All the panel edges are fixed.
J	Base & top pinned, one side pinned	The base and top are simply supported. One side is simply supported and the other side is free.
K	Top & base pinned, one side fixed	The top and base are simply supported. One of the sides is fixed and the other is free.
L	Top pinned, base & one side fixed	The top is simply supported. The base and one side are fixed. The other side is free

Table 4.1

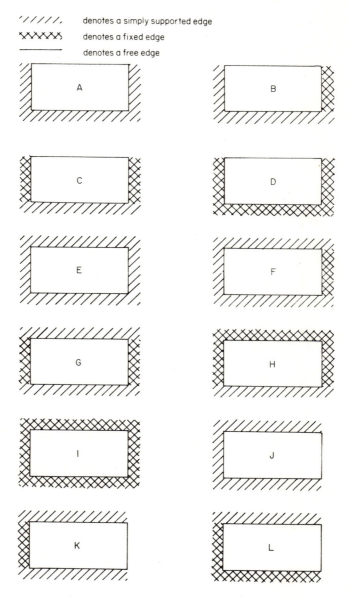

Fig. 4.1.   Diagrammatic representation of restraint cases.

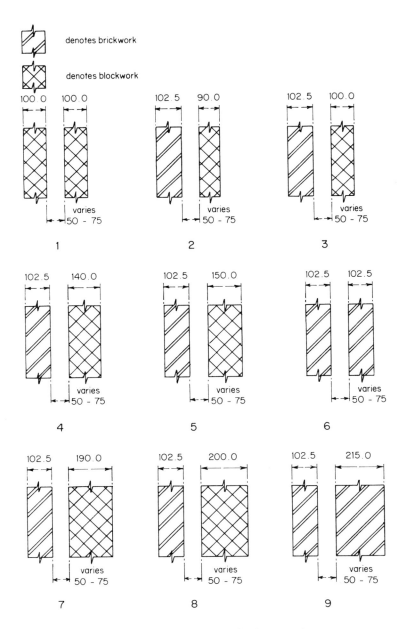

Fig. 4.2.   Wall types on design graphs
(all dimensions are in millimetres).

be halved. The wall types (see Fig. 4.2) are in order of their strength.
The curves on each design graph are in order of increasing strength of the
wall types from left to right or from bottom to top. Thus the curves
on each graph refer to wall types 1 to 9 (or less) counting from left to
right or from bottom to top.

The support conditions are referred to as simply supported (or pinned),
free and fixed.[11] A simply supported edge may be assumed when the edge is
adequately tied to the supporting structure. If it is not adequately tied
then it must be treated as a free edge. A fixed edge may be assumed where
the brickwork is continuous past, and tied to, a column or pier or is
bonded to a return wall. If there is doubt about whether fixity will be
achieved, a simple support should be assumed. It must also be noted that
the ties[16] to be used must be of adequate strength to transmit the loads
to the supporting structure which in turn must be capable of transmitting
the reactions from the panel to the ground.

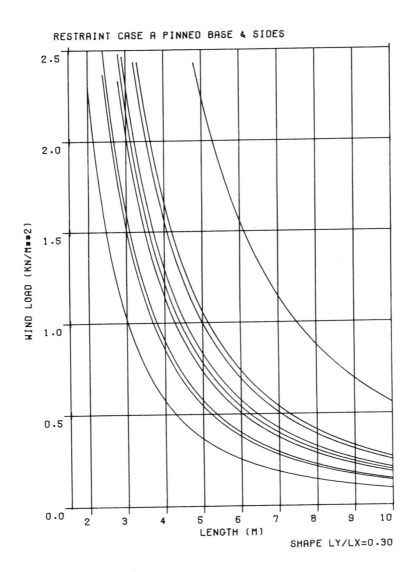

RESTRAINT CASE A PINNED BASE & SIDES

SHAPE LY/LX=0.30

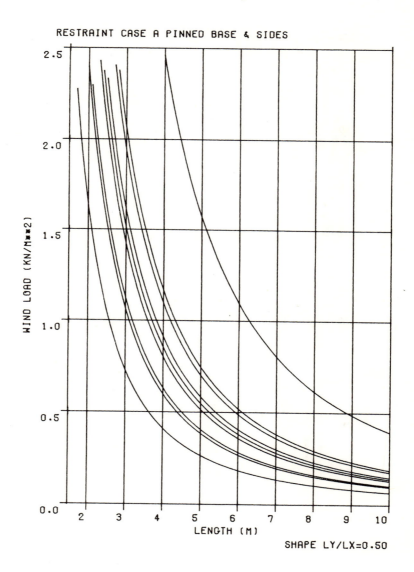

RESTRAINT CASE A PINNED BASE & SIDES

SHAPE LY/LX=0.50

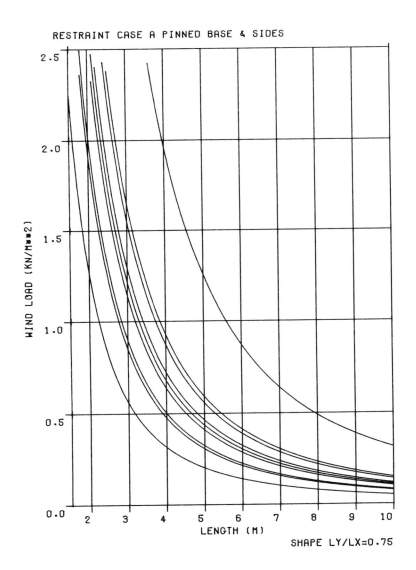

RESTRAINT CASE A PINNED BASE & SIDES

SHAPE LY/LX=0.75

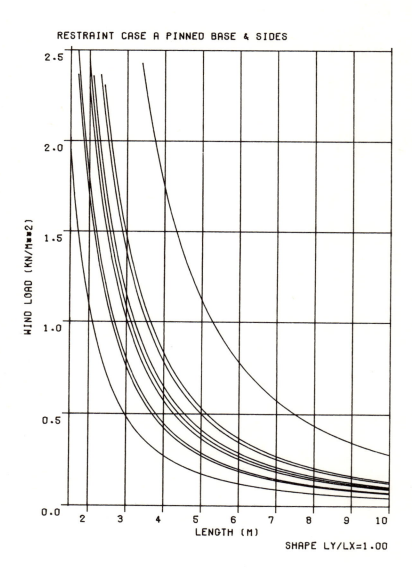

RESTRAINT CASE A PINNED BASE & SIDES

SHAPE LY/LX=1.00

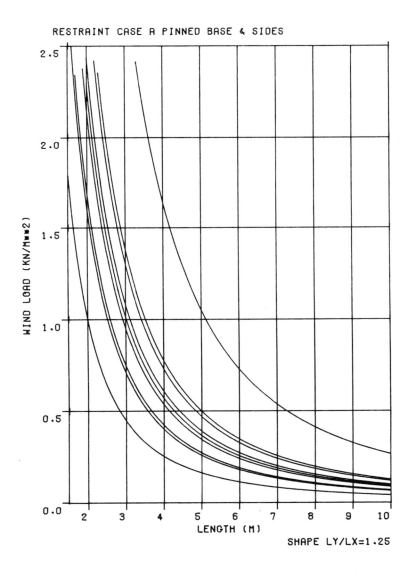

RESTRAINT CASE A PINNED BASE & SIDES

SHAPE LY/LX=1.25

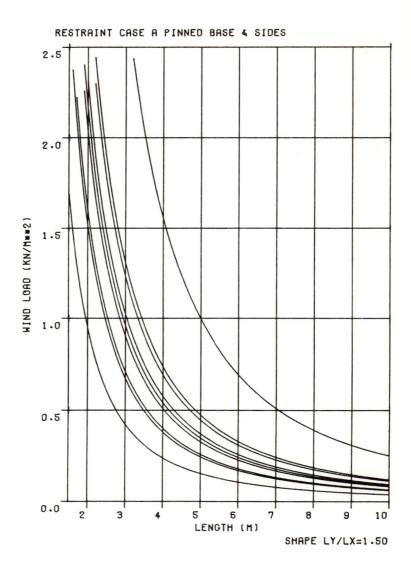

RESTRAINT CASE A PINNED BASE & SIDES

SHAPE LY/LX=1.50

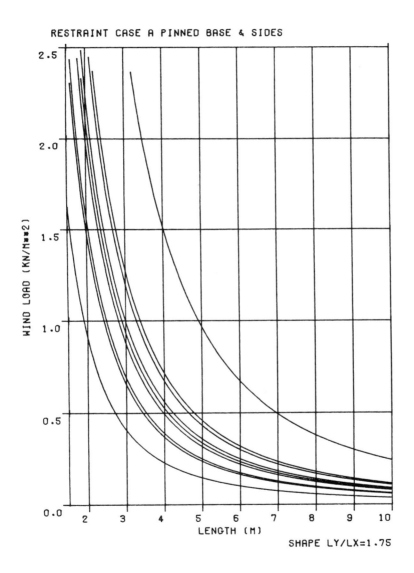

RESTRAINT CASE A PINNED BASE & SIDES

WIND LOAD (KN/M**2)

LENGTH (M)

SHAPE LY/LX=1.75

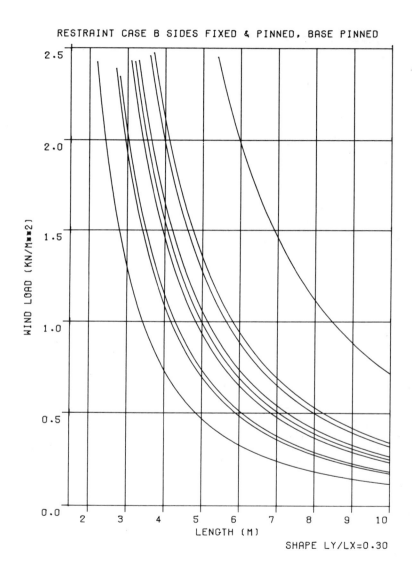

RESTRAINT CASE B SIDES FIXED & PINNED, BASE PINNED

WIND LOAD (KN/M**2)

LENGTH (M)

SHAPE LY/LX=0.30

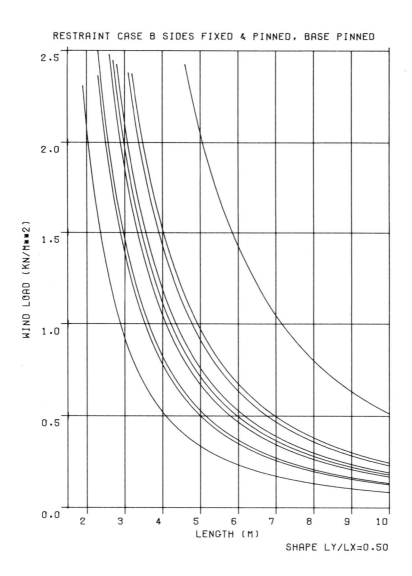

RESTRAINT CASE B SIDES FIXED & PINNED, BASE PINNED

SHAPE LY/LX=0.50

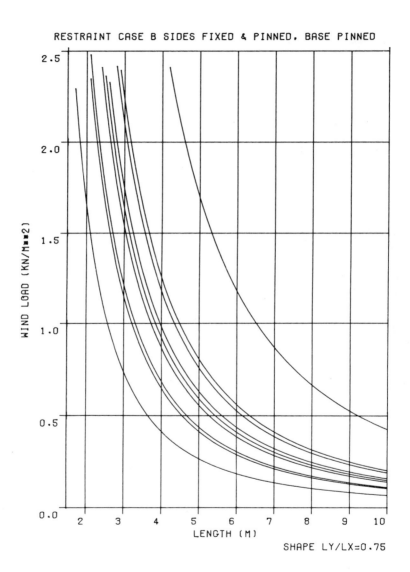

RESTRAINT CASE B SIDES FIXED & PINNED, BASE PINNED

SHAPE LY/LX=0.75

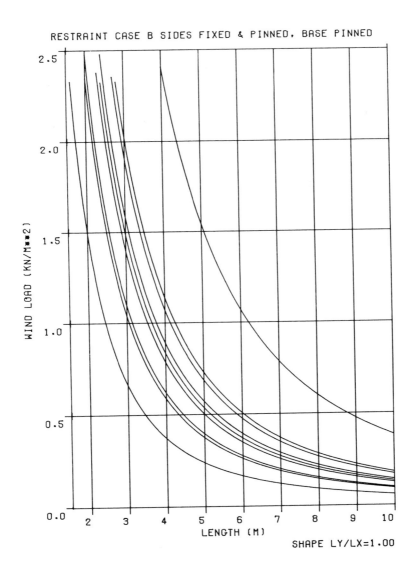

RESTRAINT CASE B SIDES FIXED & PINNED, BASE PINNED

SHAPE LY/LX=1.00

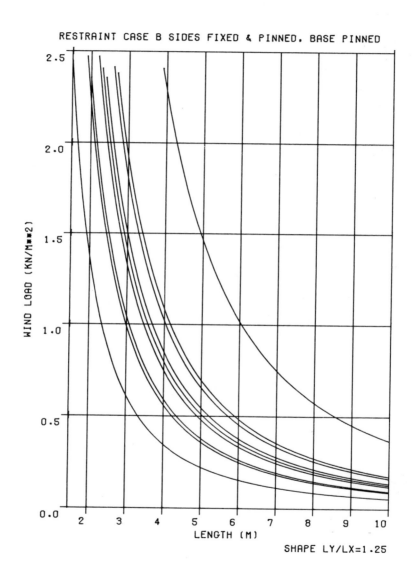

RESTRAINT CASE B SIDES FIXED & PINNED. BASE PINNED

SHAPE LY/LX=1.25

RESTRAINT CASE B SIDES FIXED & PINNED. BASE PINNED

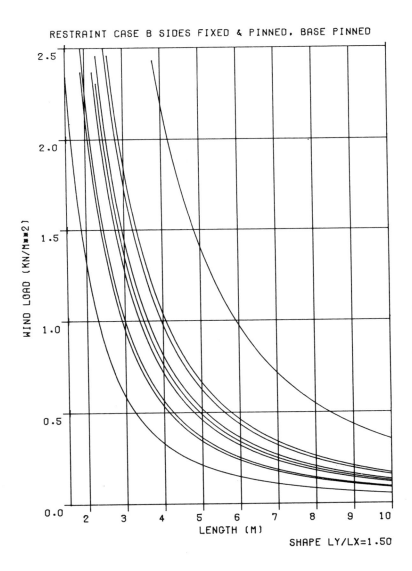

SHAPE LY/LX=1.50

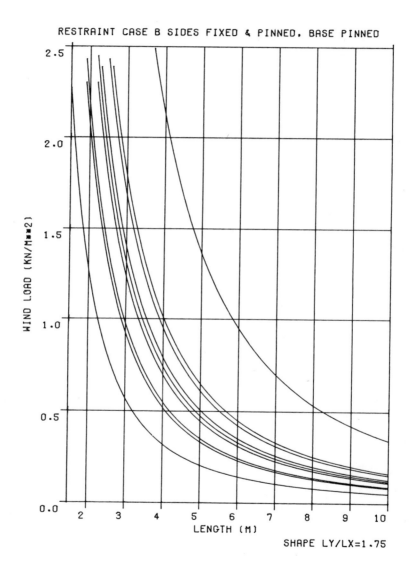

RESTRAINT CASE B SIDES FIXED & PINNED, BASE PINNED

WIND LOAD (KN/M**2)

LENGTH (M)

SHAPE LY/LX=1.75

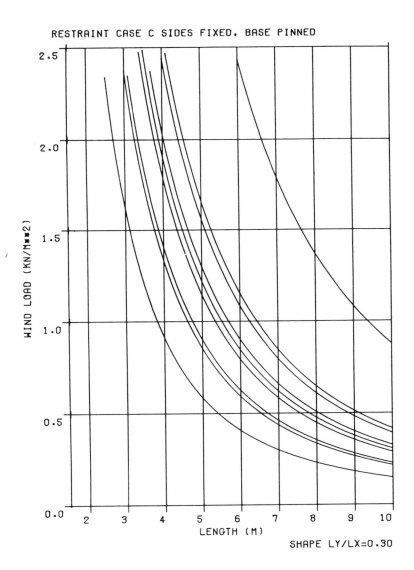

RESTRAINT CASE C SIDES FIXED, BASE PINNED

SHAPE LY/LX=0.30

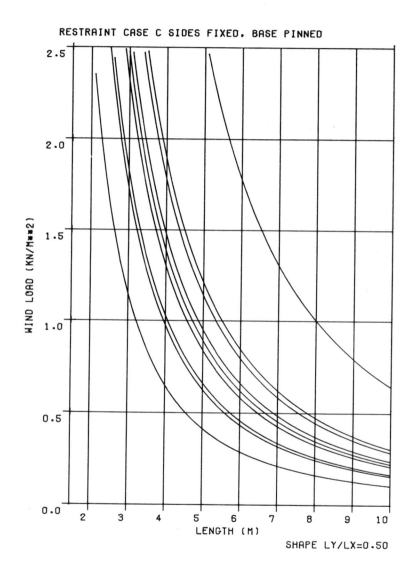

RESTRAINT CASE C SIDES FIXED. BASE PINNED

SHAPE LY/LX=0.50

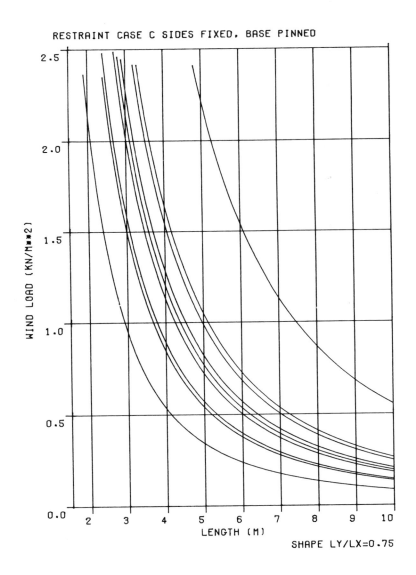

RESTRAINT CASE C SIDES FIXED, BASE PINNED

SHAPE LY/LX=0.75

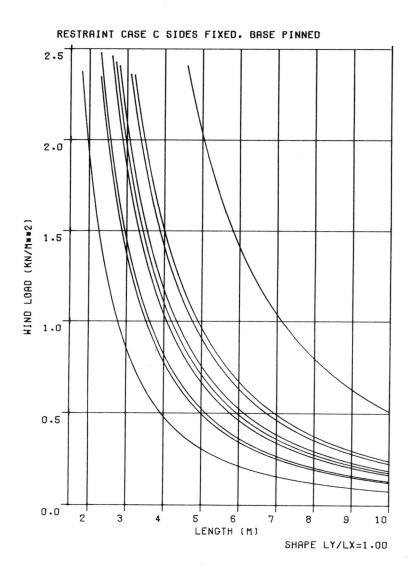

RESTRAINT CASE C SIDES FIXED, BASE PINNED

SHAPE LY/LX=1.00

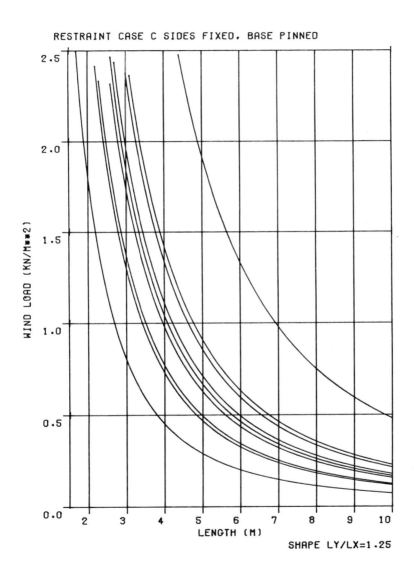

RESTRAINT CASE C SIDES FIXED, BASE PINNED

WIND LOAD (KN/M**2)

LENGTH (M)

SHAPE LY/LX=1.25

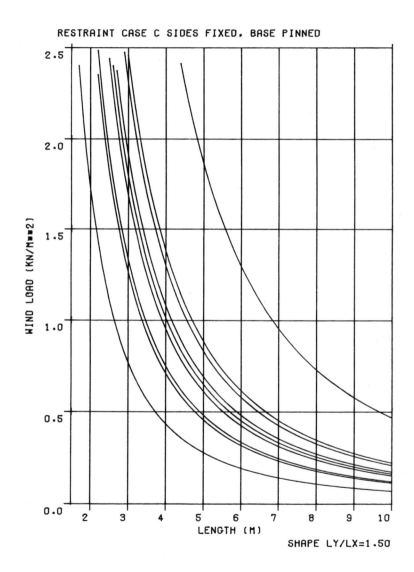

RESTRAINT CASE C SIDES FIXED, BASE PINNED

WIND LOAD (KN/M**2)

LENGTH (M)

SHAPE LY/LX=1.50

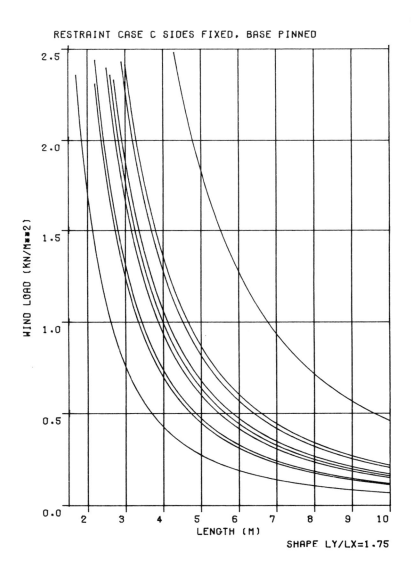

RESTRAINT CASE C SIDES FIXED, BASE PINNED

SHAPE LY/LX=1.75

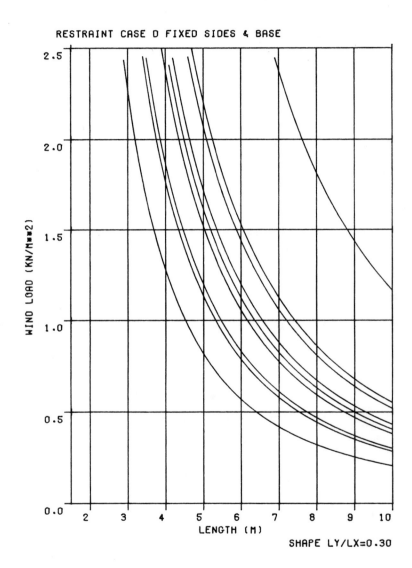

RESTRAINT CASE D FIXED SIDES & BASE

SHAPE LY/LX=0.30

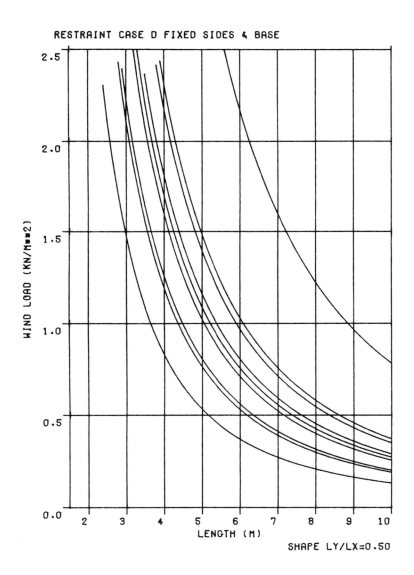

RESTRAINT CASE D FIXED SIDES & BASE

SHAPE LY/LX=0.50

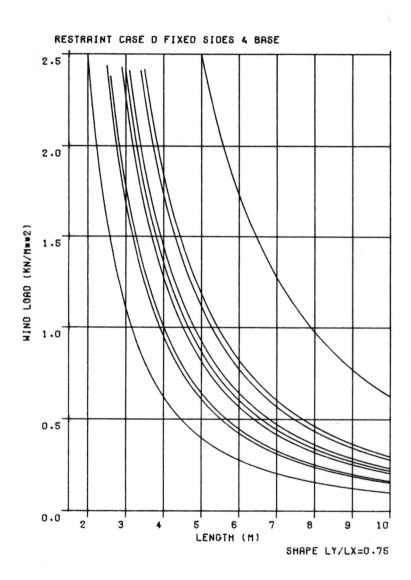

RESTRAINT CASE D FIXED SIDES & BASE

SHAPE LY/LX=0.75

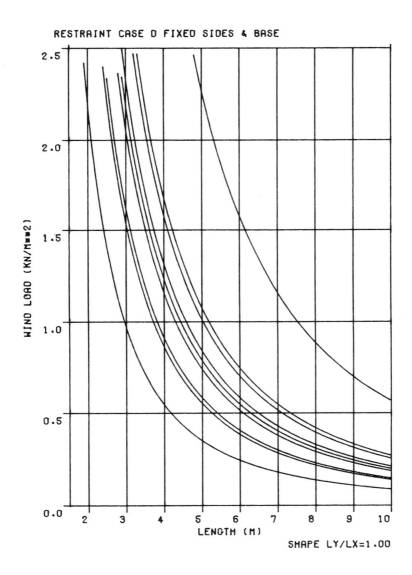

RESTRAINT CASE D FIXED SIDES & BASE

SHAPE LY/LX=1.00

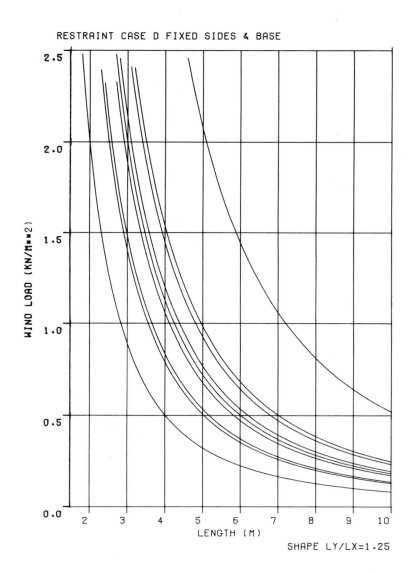

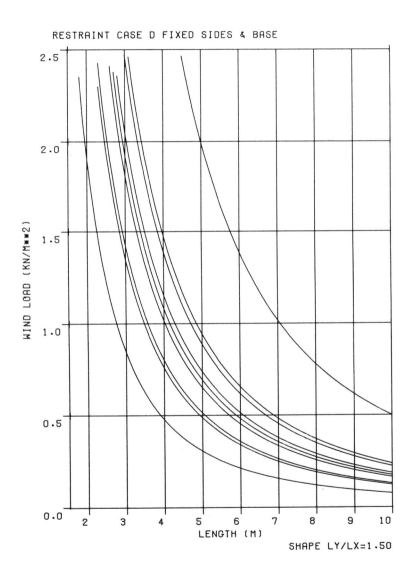

RESTRAINT CASE D FIXED SIDES & BASE

SHAPE LY/LX=1.50

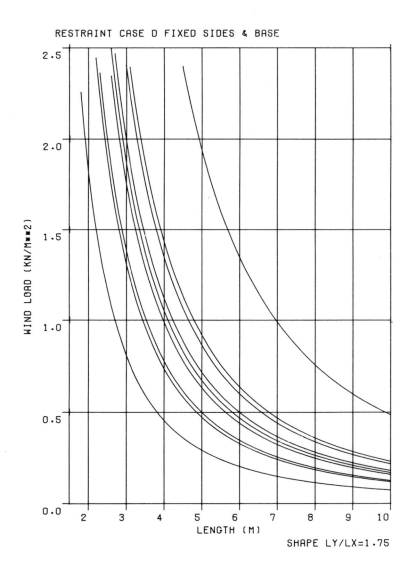

RESTRAINT CASE D FIXED SIDES & BASE

SHAPE LY/LX=1.75

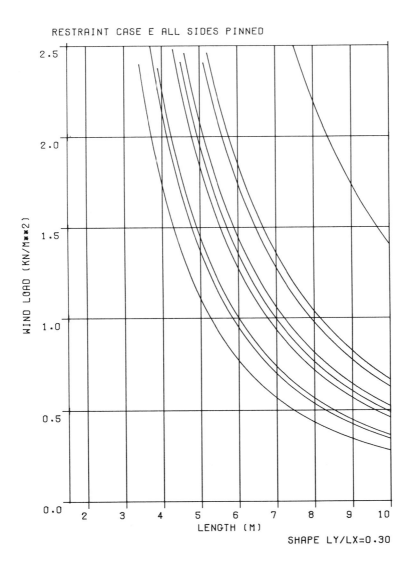

RESTRAINT CASE E ALL SIDES PINNED

WIND LOAD (KN/M**2)

LENGTH (M)

SHAPE LY/LX=0.30

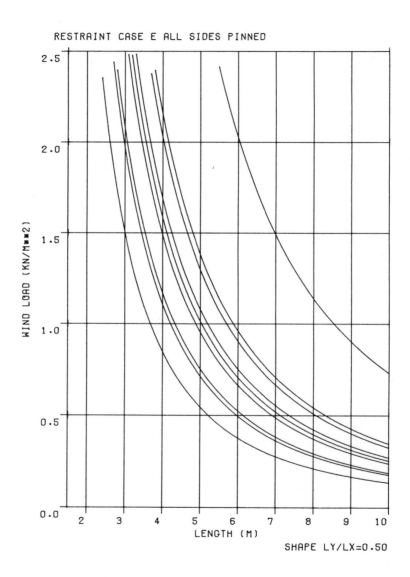

RESTRAINT CASE E ALL SIDES PINNED

SHAPE LY/LX=0.50

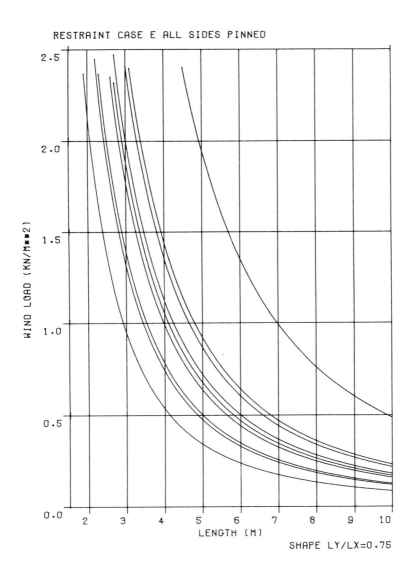

RESTRAINT CASE E ALL SIDES PINNED

SHAPE LY/LX=0.75

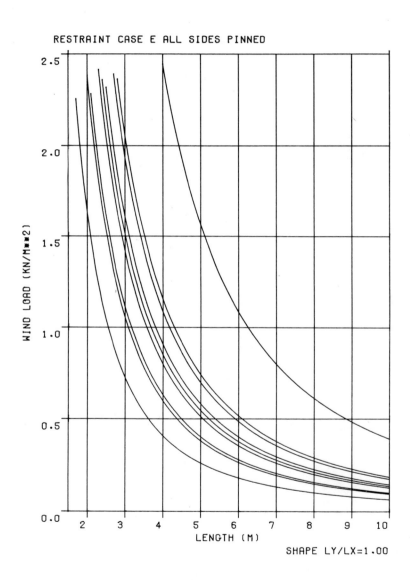

RESTRAINT CASE E ALL SIDES PINNED

WIND LOAD (KN/M**2)

LENGTH (M)

SHAPE LY/LX=1.00

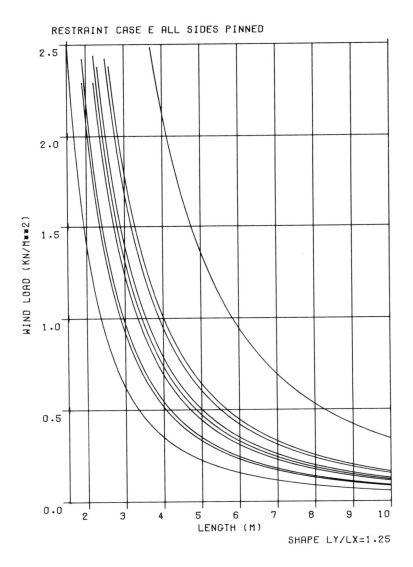

RESTRAINT CASE E ALL SIDES PINNED

SHAPE LY/LX=1.25

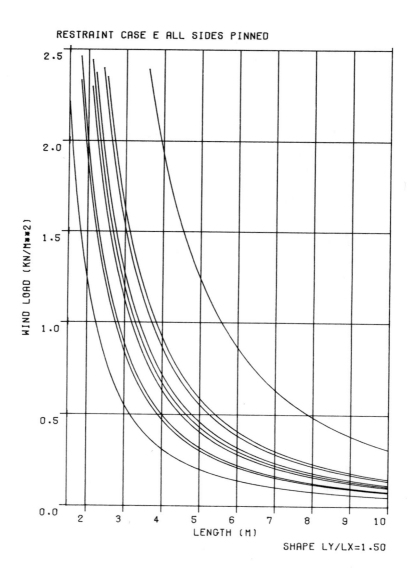

RESTRAINT CASE E ALL SIDES PINNED

SHAPE LY/LX=1.50

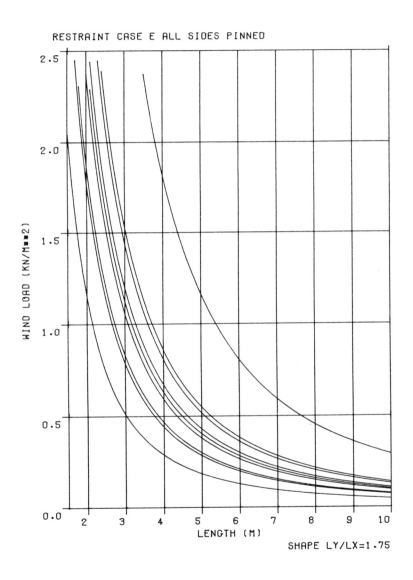

RESTRAINT CASE E ALL SIDES PINNED

WIND LOAD (KN/M**2)

LENGTH (M)

SHAPE LY/LX=1.75

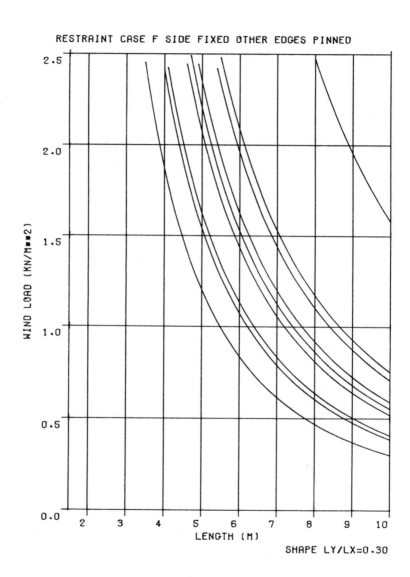

RESTRAINT CASE F SIDE FIXED OTHER EDGES PINNED

SHAPE LY/LX=0.30

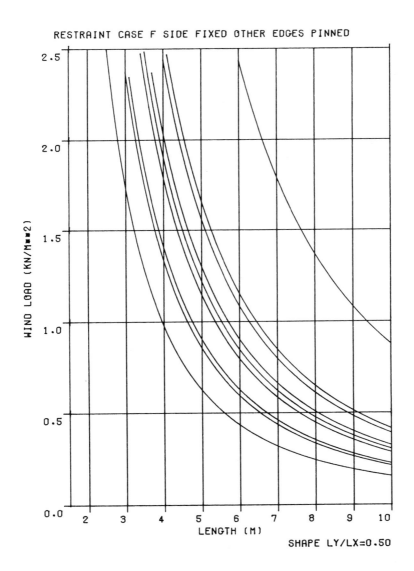

RESTRAINT CASE F SIDE FIXED OTHER EDGES PINNED

SHAPE LY/LX=0.50

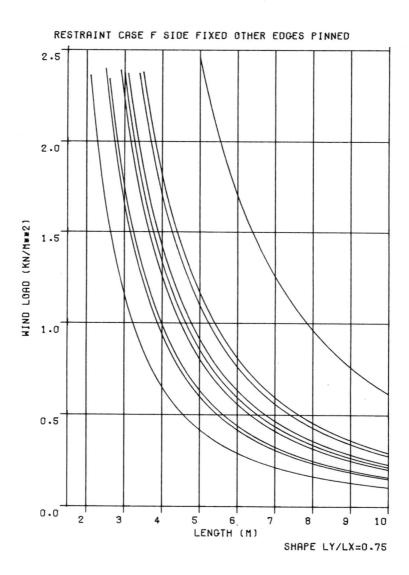

RESTRAINT CASE F SIDE FIXED OTHER EDGES PINNED

SHAPE LY/LX=0.75

RESTRAINT CASE F SIDE FIXED OTHER EDGES PINNED

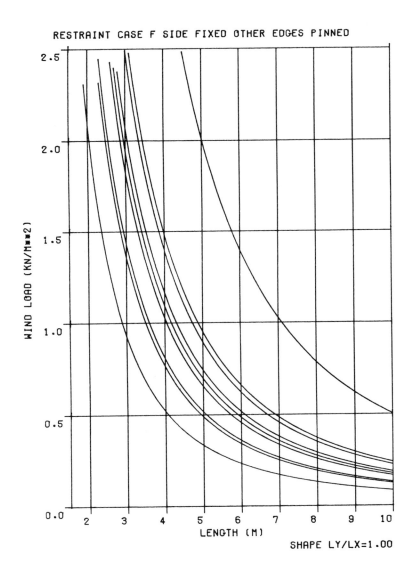

SHAPE LY/LX=1.00

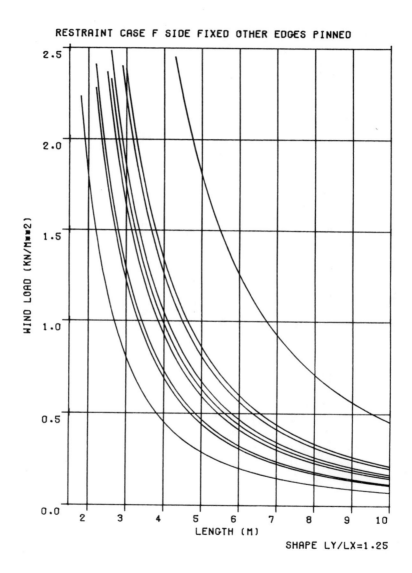

RESTRAINT CASE F SIDE FIXED OTHER EDGES PINNED

SHAPE LY/LX=1.25

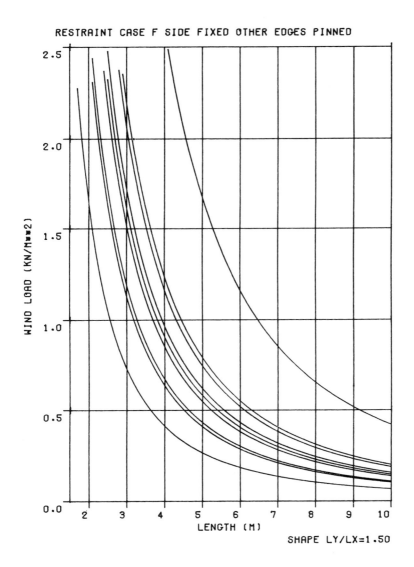

RESTRAINT CASE F SIDE FIXED OTHER EDGES PINNED

SHAPE LY/LX=1.50

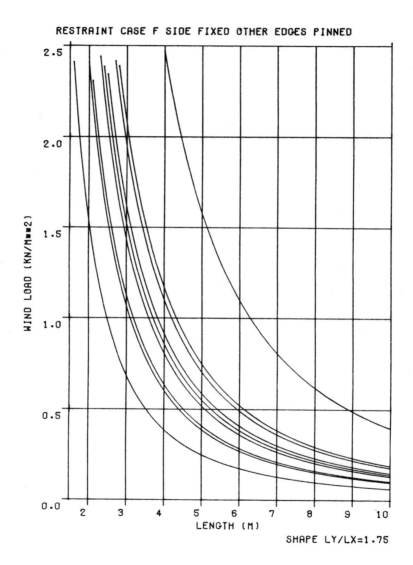

RESTRAINT CASE F SIDE FIXED OTHER EDGES PINNED

SHAPE LY/LX=1.75

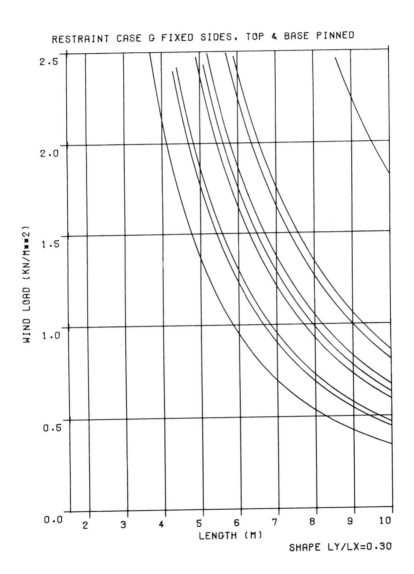

RESTRAINT CASE G FIXED SIDES, TOP & BASE PINNED

SHAPE LY/LX=0.30

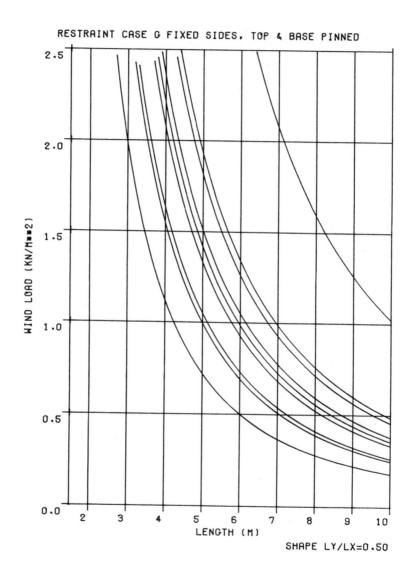

RESTRAINT CASE G FIXED SIDES, TOP & BASE PINNED

WIND LOAD (KN/M**2)

LENGTH (M)

SHAPE LY/LX=0.50

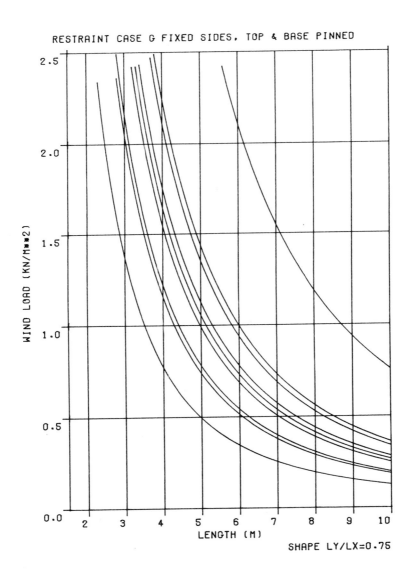

RESTRAINT CASE G FIXED SIDES, TOP & BASE PINNED

WIND LOAD (KN/M**2)

LENGTH (M)

SHAPE LY/LX=0.75

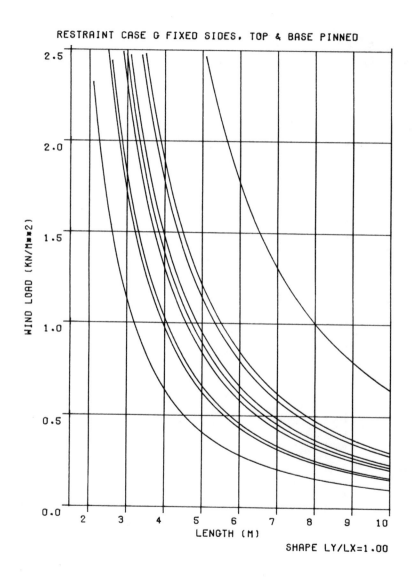

RESTRAINT CASE G FIXED SIDES, TOP & BASE PINNED

SHAPE LY/LX=1.00

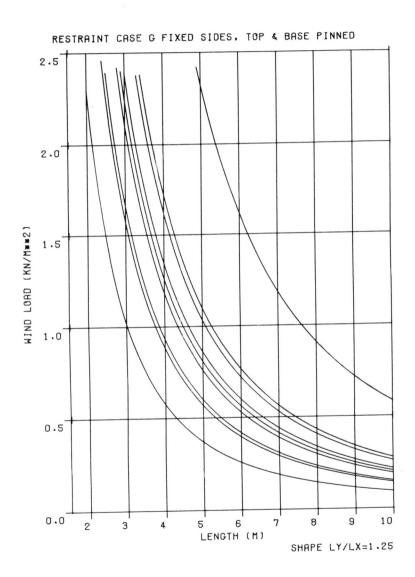

RESTRAINT CASE G FIXED SIDES, TOP & BASE PINNED

WIND LOAD (KN/M**2)

LENGTH (M)

SHAPE LY/LX=1.25

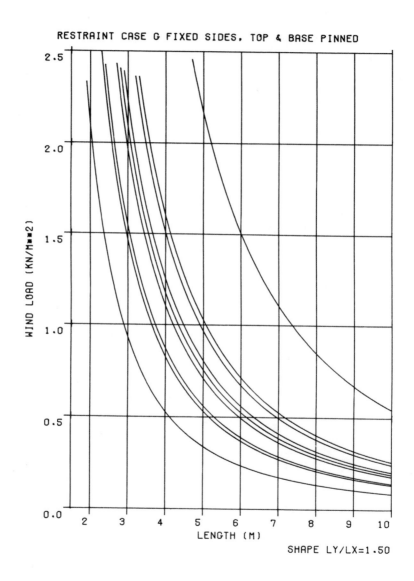

RESTRAINT CASE G FIXED SIDES, TOP & BASE PINNED

SHAPE LY/LX=1.50

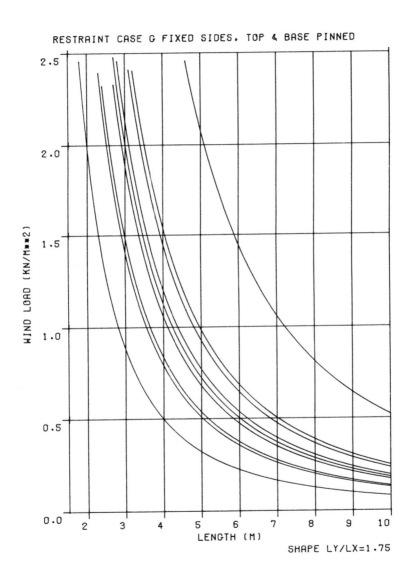

RESTRAINT CASE G FIXED SIDES, TOP & BASE PINNED

WIND LOAD (KN/M**2)

LENGTH (M)

SHAPE LY/LX=1.75

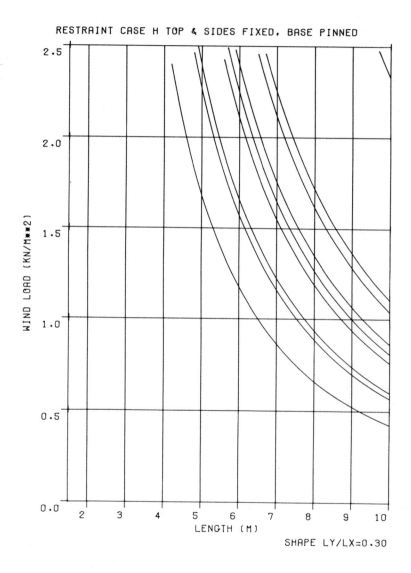

RESTRAINT CASE H TOP & SIDES FIXED, BASE PINNED

SHAPE LY/LX=0.30

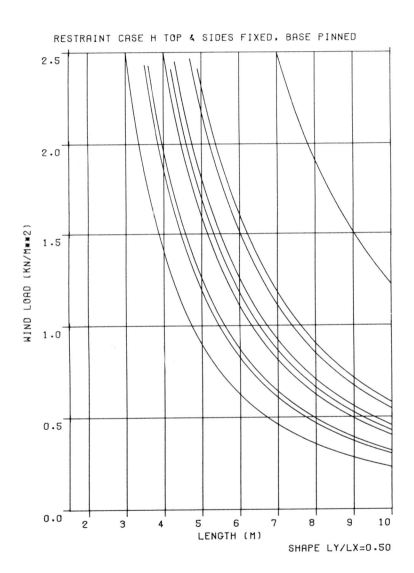

RESTRAINT CASE H TOP & SIDES FIXED, BASE PINNED

SHAPE LY/LX=0.50

RESTRAINT CASE H TOP & SIDES FIXED, BASE PINNED

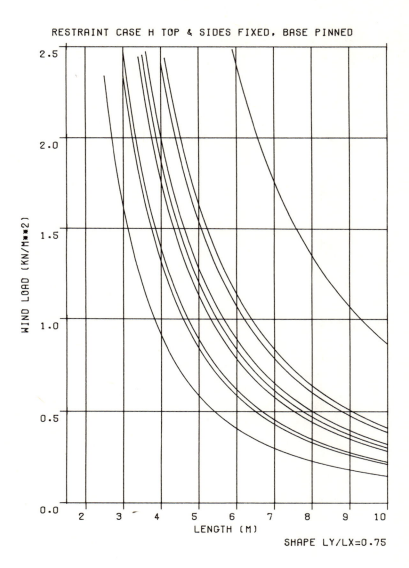

SHAPE LY/LX=0.75

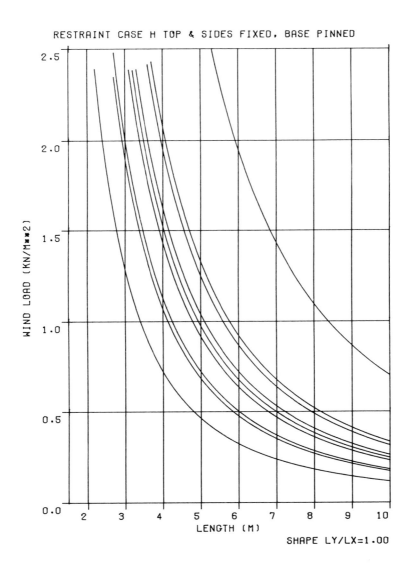

RESTRAINT CASE H TOP & SIDES FIXED, BASE PINNED

SHAPE LY/LX=1.00

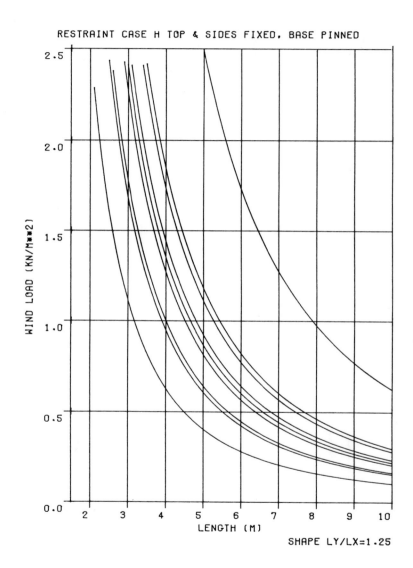

RESTRAINT CASE H TOP & SIDES FIXED, BASE PINNED

WIND LOAD (KN/M**2)

LENGTH (M)

SHAPE LY/LX=1.25

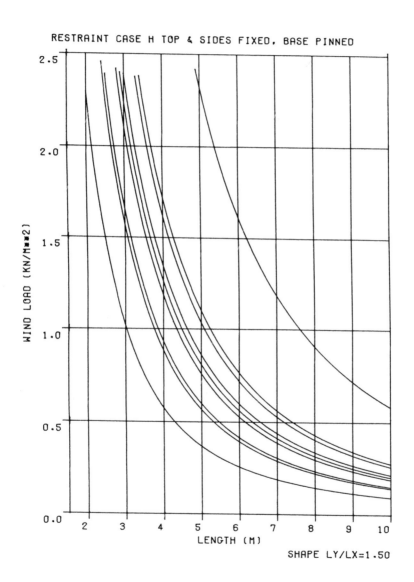

RESTRAINT CASE H TOP & SIDES FIXED, BASE PINNED

SHAPE LY/LX=1.50

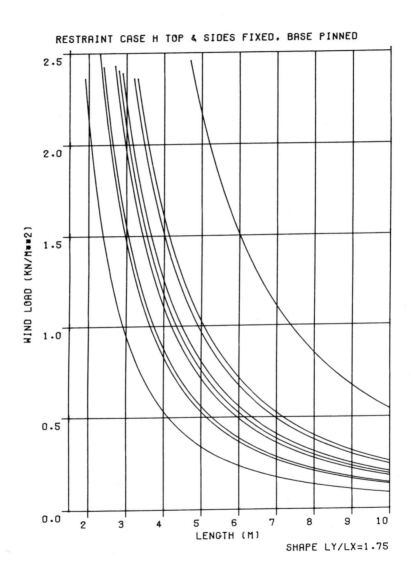

RESTRAINT CASE H TOP & SIDES FIXED, BASE PINNED

WIND LOAD (KN/M**2)

LENGTH (M)

SHAPE LY/LX=1.75

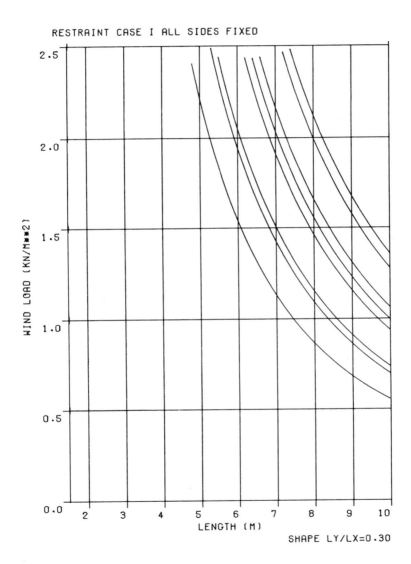

RESTRAINT CASE I ALL SIDES FIXED

SHAPE LY/LX=0.30

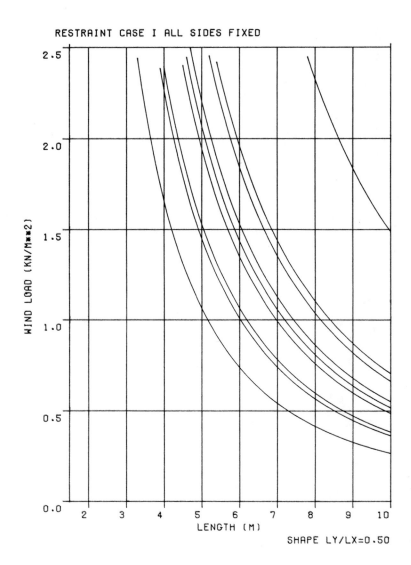

RESTRAINT CASE I ALL SIDES FIXED

SHAPE LY/LX=0.50

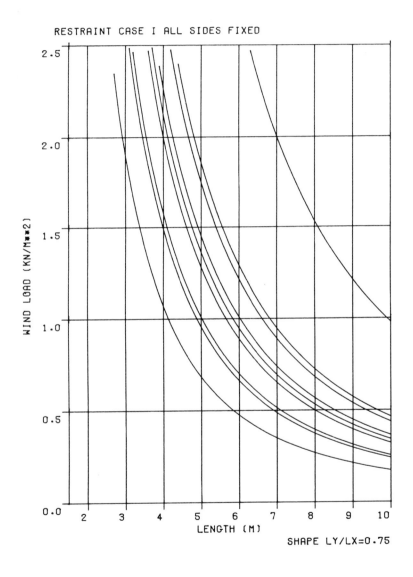

RESTRAINT CASE I ALL SIDES FIXED

WIND LOAD (KN/M**2)

LENGTH (M)

SHAPE LY/LX=0.75

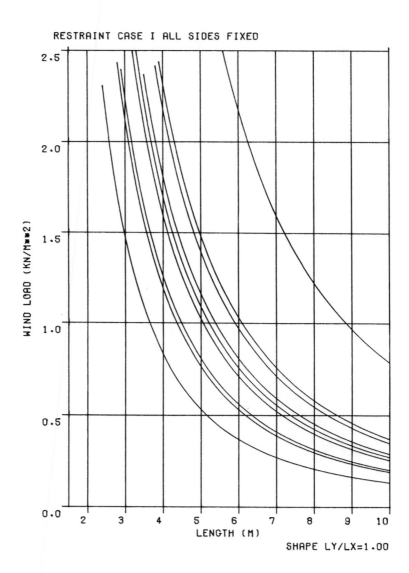

RESTRAINT CASE I ALL SIDES FIXED

SHAPE LY/LX=1.00

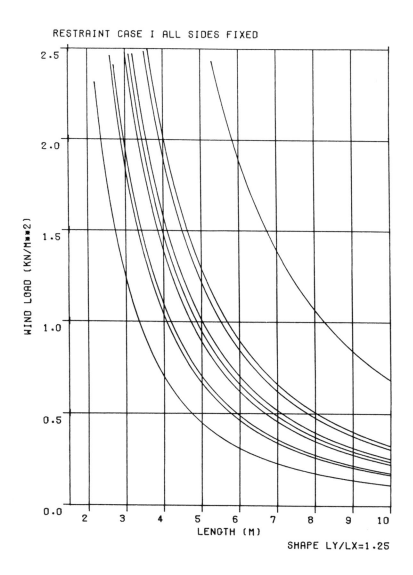

RESTRAINT CASE I ALL SIDES FIXED

SHAPE LY/LX=1.25

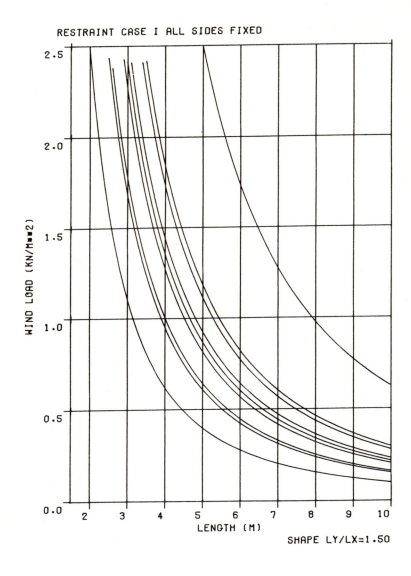

RESTRAINT CASE I ALL SIDES FIXED

SHAPE LY/LX=1.50

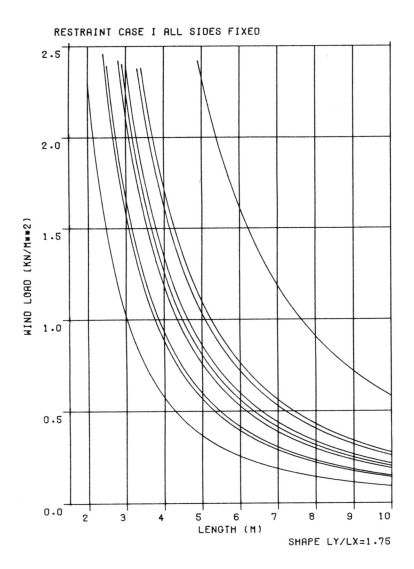

RESTRAINT CASE I ALL SIDES FIXED

SHAPE LY/LX=1.75

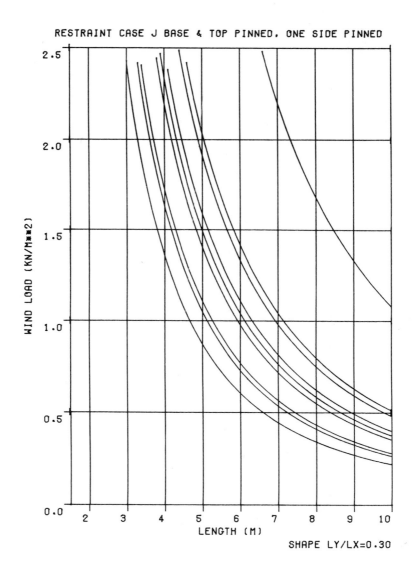

RESTRAINT CASE J BASE & TOP PINNED, ONE SIDE PINNED

SHAPE LY/LX=0.30

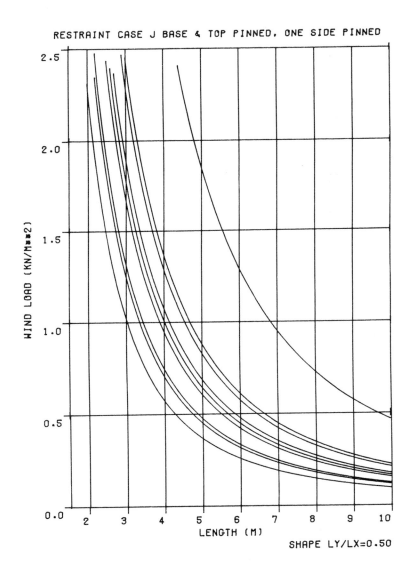

RESTRAINT CASE J BASE & TOP PINNED, ONE SIDE PINNED

WIND LOAD (KN/M**2)

LENGTH (M)

SHAPE LY/LX=0.50

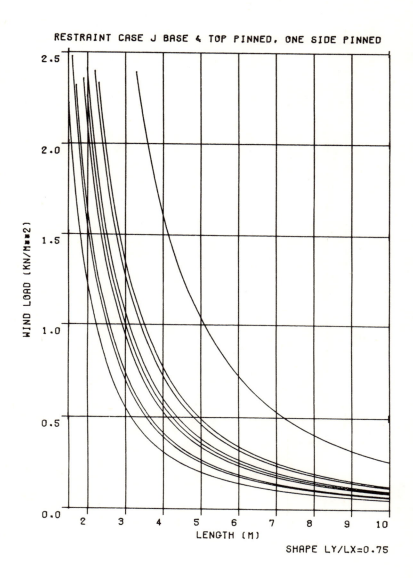

RESTRAINT CASE J BASE & TOP PINNED, ONE SIDE PINNED

SHAPE LY/LX=0.75

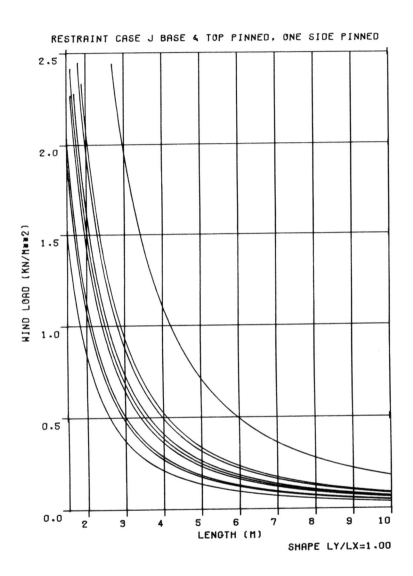

RESTRAINT CASE J BASE & TOP PINNED, ONE SIDE PINNED

SHAPE LY/LX=1.00

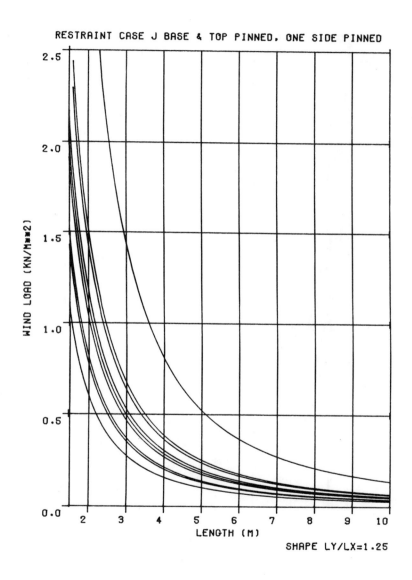

RESTRAINT CASE J BASE & TOP PINNED, ONE SIDE PINNED

SHAPE LY/LX=1.25

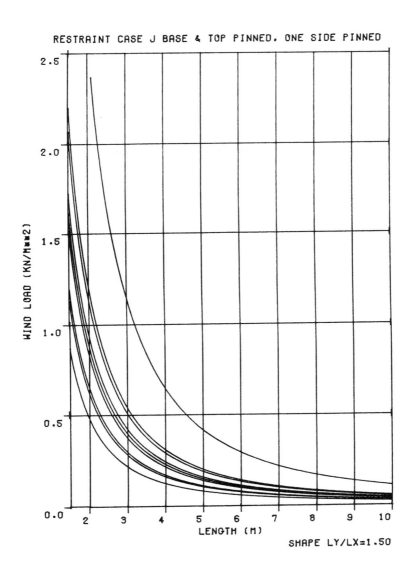

RESTRAINT CASE J BASE & TOP PINNED, ONE SIDE PINNED

WIND LOAD (KN/M**2)

LENGTH (M)

SHAPE LY/LX=1.50

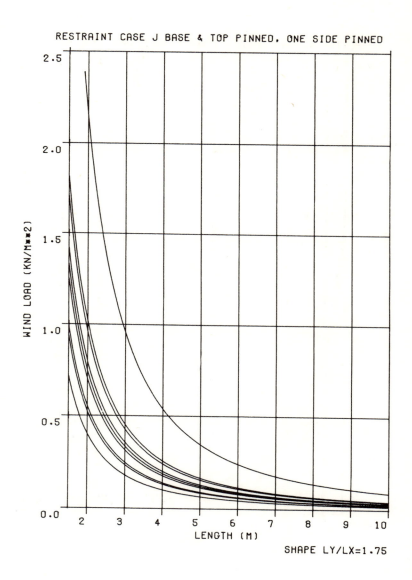

RESTRAINT CASE J BASE & TOP PINNED, ONE SIDE PINNED

WIND LOAD (KN/M**2)

LENGTH (M)

SHAPE LY/LX=1.75

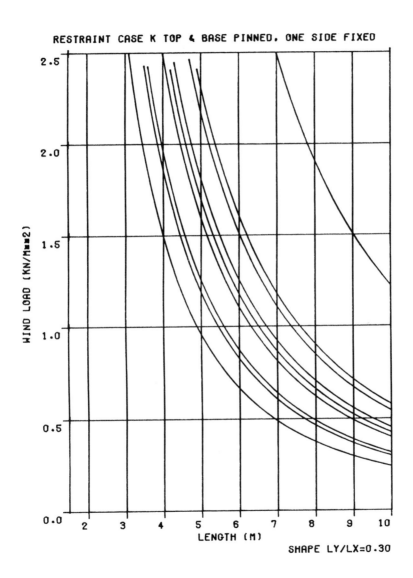

RESTRAINT CASE K TOP & BASE PINNED, ONE SIDE FIXED

WIND LOAD (KN/M**2)

LENGTH (M)

SHAPE LY/LX=0.30

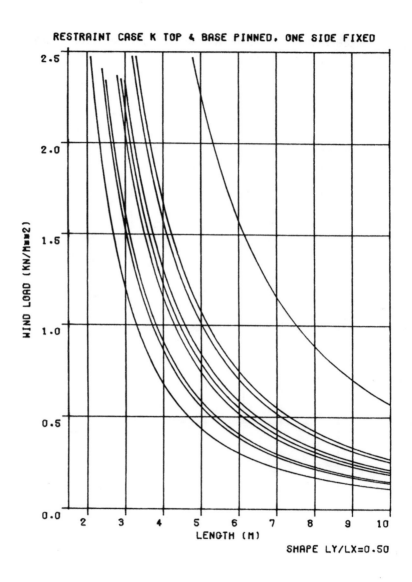

RESTRAINT CASE K TOP & BASE PINNED, ONE SIDE FIXED

SHAPE LY/LX=0.50

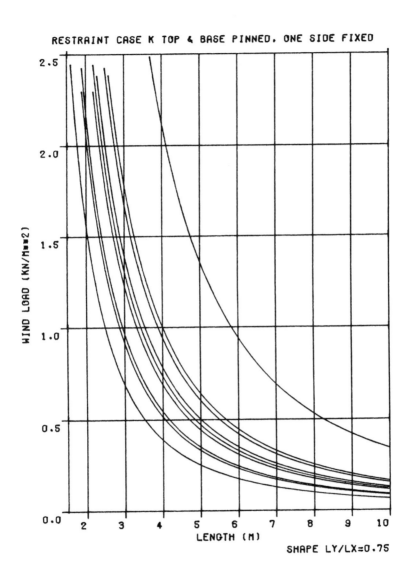

RESTRAINT CASE K TOP & BASE PINNED, ONE SIDE FIXED

SHAPE LY/LX=0.75

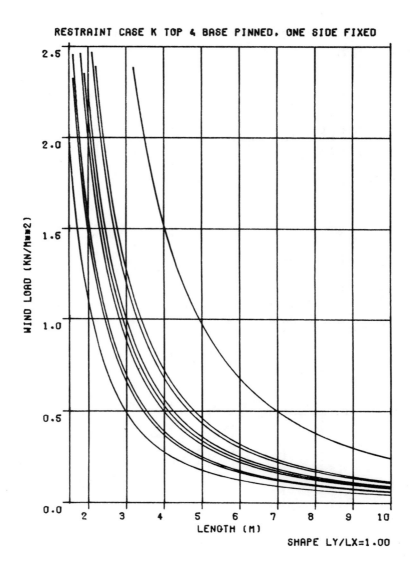

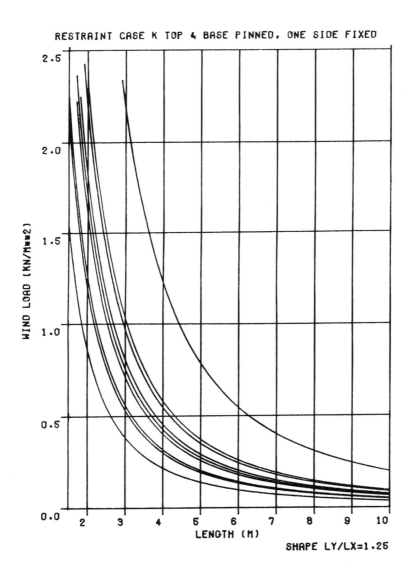

RESTRAINT CASE K TOP & BASE PINNED, ONE SIDE FIXED

SHAPE LY/LX=1.25

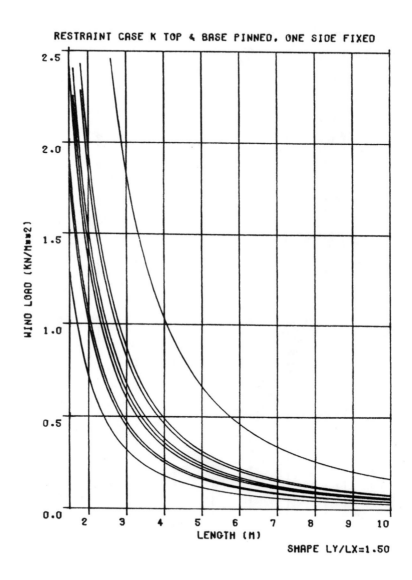

RESTRAINT CASE K TOP & BASE PINNED, ONE SIDE FIXED

WIND LOAD (KN/M**2)

LENGTH (M)

SHAPE LY/LX=1.50

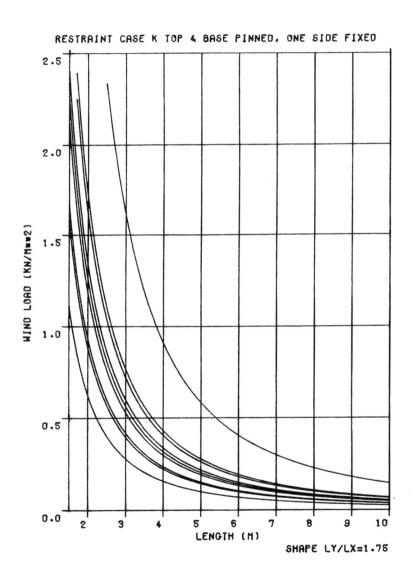

RESTRAINT CASE K TOP & BASE PINNED, ONE SIDE FIXED

WIND LOAD (KN/M**2)

LENGTH (M)

SHAPE LY/LX=1.75

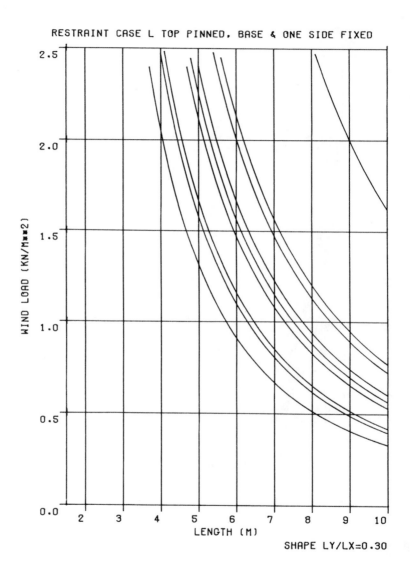

RESTRAINT CASE L TOP PINNED, BASE & ONE SIDE FIXED

SHAPE LY/LX=0.30

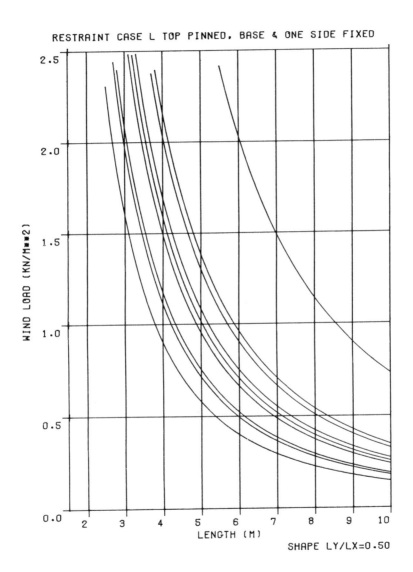

RESTRAINT CASE L TOP PINNED, BASE & ONE SIDE FIXED

WIND LOAD (KN/M**2)

LENGTH (M)

SHAPE LY/LX=0.50

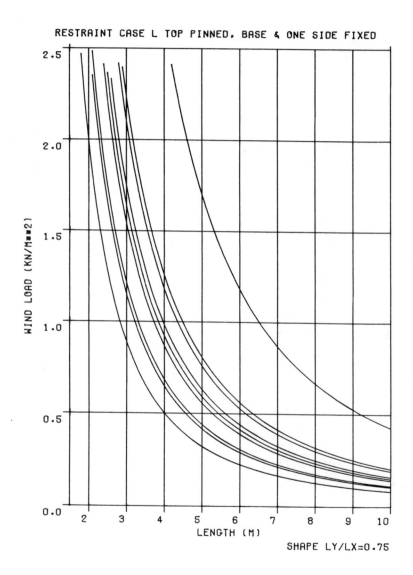

RESTRAINT CASE L TOP PINNED, BASE & ONE SIDE FIXED

SHAPE LY/LX=0.75

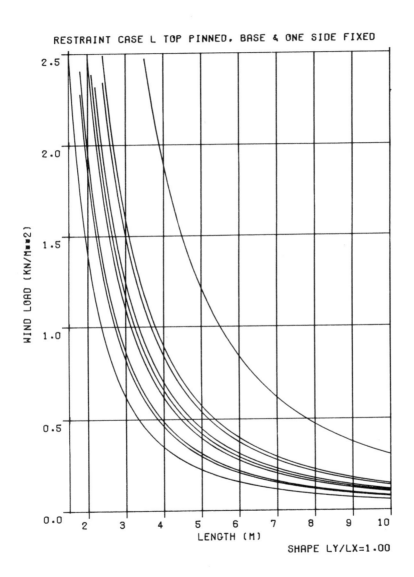

RESTRAINT CASE L TOP PINNED, BASE & ONE SIDE FIXED

WIND LOAD (KN/M**2)

LENGTH (M)

SHAPE LY/LX=1.00

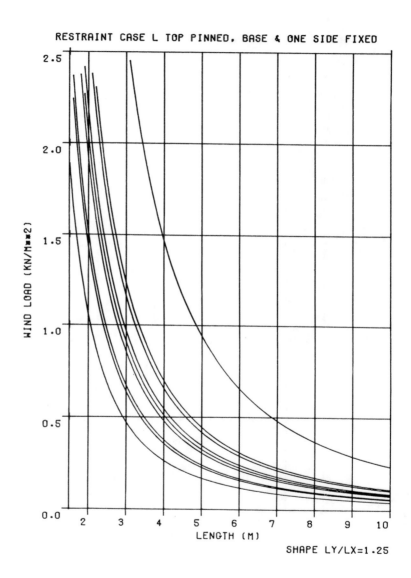

RESTRAINT CASE L TOP PINNED, BASE & ONE SIDE FIXED

WIND LOAD (KN/M**2)

LENGTH (M)

SHAPE LY/LX=1.25

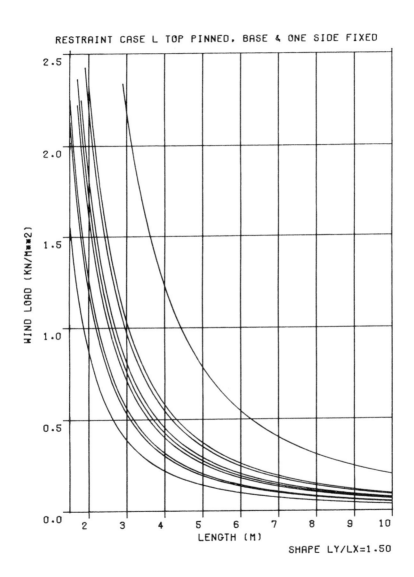

RESTRAINT CASE L TOP PINNED, BASE & ONE SIDE FIXED

SHAPE LY/LX=1.50

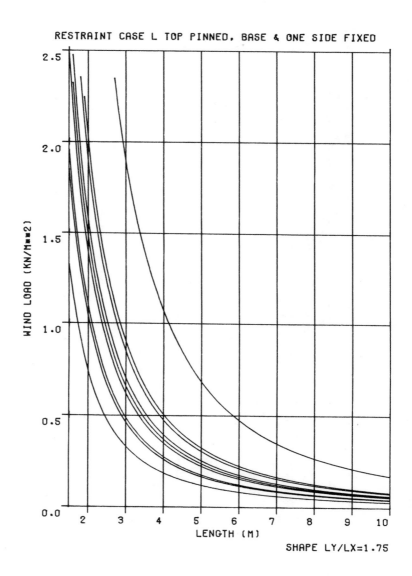

RESTRAINT CASE L TOP PINNED, BASE & ONE SIDE FIXED

SHAPE LY/LX=1.75

Chapter 5

PROGRAM INFORMATION

5.1 INTRODUCTION

A program was written to analyse panel walls subjected to lateral loading.
The panels are analysed in accordance with ref. 2 and the program produces
graphs which are given in Chapter 4. The flow chart for the program is
shown in Section 5.2. Variables used in the listing of the program and
their appropriate representations are given in Section 5.4. The format for
the data input is given in Section 5.5 and the actual data used is given in
Section 5.6.

The program inputs the wind load safety factor, the number of restraint
conditions, the number of wall types, the number of shape factors, the
maximum length of the panel required, and the increment in length to be
used. This data is then output for the user's convenience and as a check
to the graph routines. Appropriate stresses for horizontally spanning
brickwork and blockwork are then input with corresponding material strength
factors for brickwork and blockwork respectively. These stresses are
factored by the material strength factors just input. The program then
reads input data containing all the wall types to be analysed. For each
wall the thickness and modulus of elasticity of each skin are input. The
value of the modulus of elasticity is input as 1.25 for brickwork and 1.0
for blockwork. These values are not significant to the actual calculations
but serve to determine whether a brickwork or blockwork skin is being
analysed.

A counter is set at one (referring to the first restraint case) and a
restraint case is input and output. A counter for shape factors is then
set at one (referring to the first shape factor) and a shape factor and
corresponding moment coefficients for brickwork and blockwork skins are

111

input and output. Next, the graph size and axes are set using graph plotting routines. A counter is set to one for the first wall type. The variables for stresses and moment coefficients used in the equations are set to those which have been input for brickwork outer skin and blockwork inner skin. The section modulus for each skin of the panel is then calculated. The first wall type used is output as a check on the data input and a test is carried out to check that each skin uses appropriate stresses and material strength factors for the material used (a brickwork skin will use a different ultimate stress and moment coefficient to a blockwork skin). With the panel length set at 1.5, the failure load (pressure) for the two skins is determined. The failure load, length and corresponding height of the panel are output; failure load and length are stored in an array. The length of the panel is increased by the value of 'STEP' (increment in length) input in the data and a test is made to check that the panel length now set is not greater than the maximum length required, which is input as 'EMAX'. If the panel length is less than or equal to 'EMAX' then the failure load for this new panel size is calculated. Failure load, length and corresponding height are output. The failure load and length are stored in the same array as before. The process is continued until the length has exceeded the value of 'EMAX'. The curve of failure load against length is then plotted on the graph from the values in the array.

The counter for wall types ('NWALL') is increased by one and a test is made to check that this counter is less than or equal to the total number of wall types 'NWT'. If the value of 'NWALL' is less than or equal to 'NWT', the stresses and moment coefficients are reset. The process from after the first wall type was set, is now repeated for this wall type. If the counter for wall types is not less than or equal to the total number of wall types 'NWT', all the wall types have been plotted for one value of shape factor and one set of restraint conditions. Therefore the titles are now printed and cross lines are drawn on the first graph.

The counter for shape factors 'MSH' is increased by one and a test is made to check the value of 'MSH'. If the value of 'MSH' is less than or equal to 'MAXAPE' (total number of shape factors) then the next shape factor and corresponding moment coefficients are input. The process from where the first shape factor was input is repeated until the counter for shape factors 'MSH' exceeds the value of 'MAXAPE'.

The counter for the restraint cases 'NRES' is then increased by one and a test made to check that the number of restraint cases 'NRES' is less than or equal to the total number of restraint cases to be used, 'NRE'. If 'NRES' is less than or equal to 'NRE', a new restraint case is input and the process is repeated from where the first restraint case was input until the counter for restraint cases exceeds 'NRE'. The program is by then finished and a set of graphs produced for each shape factor for each restraint case (as seen in Chapter 4).

When running programs, care must be taken to ensure that enough time, paper and storage space (the program uses approximately 20 kilobytes of storage) are specified. The time used depends upon the number of graphs to be plotted and the interval in length 'STEP' used.

The values of the moment coefficients used in the program data are taken from ref. 2 and are for walls as described in Table 3.1.

5.2   FLOW CHART

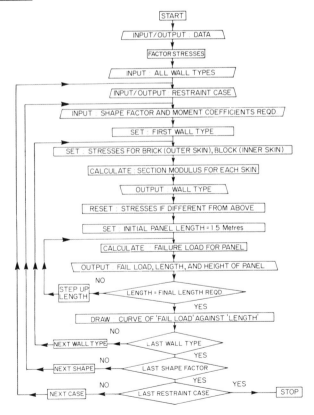

5.3   PROGRAM LISTING

The program listing is the copyright of the author. Any reader interested
in using the program should contact the author.

5.4   VARIABLES USED IN PROGRAM

Symbol	Type	Meaning
AMO(2)	real	initial bending moment coefficients input to program
AO(2)	real	bending moment coefficients used in equations
AX(2)	real	array used for graph labels
AY(2)	real	array used for graph labels
B(2)	real	initial stresses input to program
BUFFER(2)	real	used for storing value of shape for graph plot
E(2,10)	real	modulus of elasticity of brick/block
EENT	real	length of panel
EMAX	real	maximum length of panel
F(2)	real	stresses used in equations
GALL(150)	real	values of wind load for graph plotting
GAM(2)	real	partial safety factors for material strength
GAMF	real	partial safety factor for design loads
GENT(150)	real	values of length for graph plotting
H	real	height of panel
LOAD	real	fail wind load
MAXAPE	integer	number of shape factors used for each restraint case
MSH	integer	counter for shape factors
NRE	integer	number of restraint cases
NRES	integer	counter for restraint cases
NWALL	integer	counter for wall types
NWT	integer	number of wall types
STEP	integer	increment in length of panel
X1	real	used in graphplotting routines for crosslines on graphs
X2	real	used in graphplotting routines for crosslines on graphs
X2A	real	used in graphplotting routines for crosslines on graphs
Y1	real	used in graphplotting routines for crosslines on graphs
Y2	real	used in graphplotting routines for crosslines on graphs
Z(2)	real	section modulus of each skin

5.5 DATA INPUT (FORMAT)

Wind load safety factor (GAMF)	* * * *	No. of restraint con- ditions (NRE)	* * * *	No. of wall types (NWT)	* * * *	Max No. of shape factors (MAXAPE)	* * * *	Max length of panel (m) (EMAX)	* * * *	Step reqd. (m) (STEP)

	v		v		v		v		v		N/L
real		integer		integer		integer		real		real	

STRESSES :
(N/MM**2)

Brickwork horizontally spanning (B(1))	* * *	Brick stress material factor (GAM(1))	* * *	Blockwork horizontally spanning (B(2))	* * *	Block stress material factor (GAM(2))

	v		v		v		N/L

all real numbers

WALL TYPES: Maximum No. (NWT)

OUTER SKIN		INNER SKIN		Note:
* Thickness * * (mm) * (TH(1,J))	* Elastic * Modulus * (KN/mm**2) * (E(1,J))	* Thickness * * (mm) * (TH(2,J))	* Elastic * Modulus *(KN/mm**2)* (E(2,J))	* * * *	Elastic Modulus Brickwork = 1.25 Blockwork = 1.00

	v		v		v		N/L
	v		v		v		N/L
	v		v		v		N/L
	v		v		v		N/L
	v		v		v		N/L
	v		v		v		N/L
	v		v		v		N/L
	v		v		v		N/L
	v		v		v		N/L
	v		v		v		N/L
	v		v		v		N/L
	v		v		v		N/L

all real numbers

NOTES   Data given in boxes   v   means space character
         Ignore blank lines   N/L means newline character

RESTRAINT CASE AND CORRESPONDING DATA
Maximum No. (NRE)

RESTRAINT CASE :

name in characters (maximum number 56)

SHAPE FACTORS AND CORRESPONDING BENDING MOMENT COEFFICIENTS.
MAXIMUM NO. (MAXAPE)

Shape factor   * Horizontal moment   * Horizontal moment
                * coefficient for   * coefficient for
                * brickwork   * blockwork

	v		v		N/L
	v		v		N/L
	v		v		N/L
	v		v		N/L
	v		v		N/L
	v		v		N/L
	v		v		N/L
	v		v		N/L
	v		v		N/L
	v		v		N/L
	v		v		N/L
	v		v		N/L

all real numbers

5.6 DATA INPUT

Wind load safety factor (GAMF)	* * * * *	No. of restraint con-ditions (NRE)	* * * * *	No. of wall types (NWT)	* * * * *	Max No. of shape factors (MAXAPE)	* * * * *	Max length of panel (m) (EMAX)	* * * * *	Step reqd. (m) (STEP)

1.2	v	12	v	9	v	7	v	10.0	v	0.1	N/L
real		integer		integer		integer		real		real	

STRESSES : (N/MM**2)	Brickwork horizontally spanning (B(1))	* Brick stress * material * factor * (GAM(1))	* Blockwork * horizontally * spanning * (B(2))	* Block stress * material * factor * (GAM(2))

	1.1	v	3.5	v	0.45	v	3.5	N/L

all real numbers

WALL TYPES: Maximum No. (NWT)	OUTER SKIN		INNER SKIN			Note:
	* Thickness * * (mm) * *(TH(1,J))	* Elastic * Modulus * (KN/mm**2)* * (E(1,J))	* Thickness * (mm) * (TH(2,J))	* Elastic * Modulus * (KN/mm**2)* * (E(2,J))	* * * *	Elastic Modulus Brickwork = 1.25 Blockwork = 1.00

100.0	v	1.0	v	100.0	v	1.0	N/L
102.5	v	1.25	v	90.0	v	1.0	N/L
102.5	v	1.25	v	100.0	v	1.0	N/L
102.5	v	1.25	v	140.0	v	1.0	N/L
102.5	v	1.25	v	150.0	v	1.0	N/L
102.5	v	1.25	v	102.5	v	1.25	N/L
102.5	v	1.25	v	190.0	v	1.0	N/L
102.5	v	1.25	v	200.0	v	1.0	N/L
102.5	v	1.25	v	215.0	v	1.25	N/L
	v		v		v		N/L
	v		v		v		N/L
	v		v		v		N/L

all real numbers

NOTES Data given in boxes   v   means space character
       Ignore blank lines   N/L means newline character

RESTRAINT CASE AND CORRESPONDING DATA
Maximum No. (NRE)

RESTRAINT CASE : | RESTRAINT CASE A PINNED BASE & SIDES |

name in characters (maximum number 56)

SHAPE FACTORS AND CORRESPONDING BENDING MOMENT COEFFICIENTS.
MAXIMUM NO. (MAXAPE)

Shape factor	*	Horizontal moment coefficient for brickwork	*	Horizontal moment coefficient for blockwork	
0.3	v	0.0442727	v	0.0388889	N/L
0.5	v	0.0629091	v	0.0543333	N/L
0.75	v	0.0789091	v	0.0707778	N/L
1.0	v	0.0882727	v	0.0813333	N/L
1.25	v	0.0942727	v	0.0888889	N/L
1.5	v	0.0992727	v	0.0938889	N/L
1.75	v	0.1022727	v	0.0978889	N/L
	v		v		N/L
	v		v		N/L
	v		v		N/L
	v		v		N/L
	v		v		N/L

all real numbers

RESTRAINT CASE AND CORRESPONDING DATA
Maximum No. (NRE)

RESTRAINT CASE : | RESTRAINT CASE B SIDES FIXED & PINNED, BASE PINNED |

name in characters (maximum number 56)

SHAPE FACTORS AND CORRESPONDING BENDING MOMENT COEFFICIENTS.
MAXIMUM NO. (MAXAPE)

Shape factor	*	Horizontal moment coefficient for brickwork	*	Horizontal moment coefficient for blockwork	
0.3	v	0.0346364	v	0.0304444	N/L
0.5	v	0.0482727	v	0.0428889	N/L
0.75	v	0.0582727	v	0.0538889	N/L
1.0	v	0.0642727	v	0.0598889	N/L
1.25	v	0.0676364	v	0.0648889	N/L
1.5	v	0.0706364	v	0.0678889	N/L
1.75	v	0.0726364	v	0.0698889	N/L
	v		v		N/L
	v		v		N/L
	v		v		N/L
	v		v		N/L

all real numbers

RESTRAINT CASE AND CORRESPONDING DATA
Maximum No. (NRE)

RESTRAINT CASE   : | RESTRAINT CASE C SIDES FIXED, BASE PINNED

name in characters (maximum number 56)

SHAPE FACTORS AND CORRESPONDING BENDING MOMENT COEFFICIENTS.
MAXIMUM NO. (MAXAPE)

Shape factor	*	Horizontal moment coefficient for brickwork	*	Horizontal moment coefficient for blockwork	
0.3	v	0.0282727	v	0.0244444	N/L
0.5	v	0.0386364	v	0.0344444	N/L
0.75	v	0.0446364	v	0.0418889	N/L
1.0	v	0.0486364	v	0.0464444	N/L
1.25	v	0.0516364	v	0.0494444	N/L
1.5	v	0.0530000	v	0.0514444	N/L
1.75	v	0.0540000	v	0.0524444	N/L
	v		v		N/L
	v		v		N/L
	v		v		N/L
	v		v		N/L

all real numbers

RESTRAINT CASE AND CORRESPONDING DATA
Maximum No. (NRE)

RESTRAINT CASE : | RESTRAINT CASE D FIXED SIDES & BASE |

name in characters (maximum number 56)

SHAPE FACTORS AND CORRESPONDING BENDING MOMENT COEFFICIENTS.
MAXIMUM NO. (MAXAPE)

Shape factor	*	Horizontal moment coefficient for brickwork	*	Horizontal moment coefficient for blockwork	
0.3	v	0.0212727	v	0.0174444	N/L
0.5	v	0.0316364	v	0.0268889	N/L
0.75	v	0.0396364	v	0.0358889	N/L
1.0	v	0.0436364	v	0.0408889	N/L
1.25	v	0.0476364	v	0.0444444	N/L
1.5	v	0.0496364	v	0.0468889	N/L
1.75	v	0.051	v	0.0488889	N/L
	v		v		N/L
	v		v		N/L
	v		v		N/L
	v		v		N/L

all real numbers

RESTRAINT CASE AND CORRESPONDING DATA
Maximum No. (NRE)

RESTRAINT CASE : | RESTRAINT CASE E ALL SIDES PINNED |

                  name in characters (maximum number 56)

SHAPE FACTORS AND CORRESPONDING BENDING MOMENT COEFFICIENTS.
MAXIMUM NO. (MAXAPE)

Shape factor	*	Horizontal moment coefficient for brickwork	*	Horizontal moment coefficient for blockwork	
0.3	v	0.0176364	v	0.0128889	N/L
0.5	v	0.0339091	v	0.0263333	N/L
0.75	v	0.0509091	v	0.0417778	N/L
1.0	v	0.0632727	v	0.0547778	N/L
1.25	v	0.0729091	v	0.0637778	N/L
1.5	v	0.0799091	v	0.0717778	N/L
1.75	v	0.0852727	v	0.0777778	N/L
	v		v		N/L
	v		v		N/L
	v		v		N/L
	v		v		N/L

                  all real numbers

RESTRAINT CASE AND CORRESPONDING DATA
Maximum No. (NRE)

RESTRAINT CASE : | RESTRAINT CASE F SIDE FIXED OTHER EDGES PINNED |

name in characters (maximum number 56)

SHAPE FACTORS AND CORRESPONDING BENDING MOMENT COEFFICIENTS.
MAXIMUM NO. (MAXAPE)

Shape factor	*	Horizontal moment coefficient for brickwork	*	Horizontal moment coefficient for blockwork	
0.3	v	0.0156364	v	0.0118889	N/L
0.5	v	0.0282727	v	0.0228889	N/L
0.75	v	0.0402727	v	0.0343333	N/L
1.0	v	0.0492727	v	0.0428889	N/L
1.25	v	0.0546364	v	0.0493333	N/L
1.5	v	0.0592727	v	0.0543333	N/L
1.75	v	0.0626364	v	0.0578889	N/L
	v		v		N/L
	v		v		N/L
	v		v		N/L
	v		v		N/L

all real numbers

RESTRAINT CASE AND CORRESPONDING DATA
Maximum No. (NRE)

RESTRAINT CASE : | RESTRAINT CASE G FIXED SIDES, TOP & BASE PINNED |

name in characters (maximum number 56)

SHAPE FACTORS AND CORRESPONDING BENDING MOMENT COEFFICIENTS.
MAXIMUM NO. (MAXAPE)

Shape factor	*	Horizontal moment coefficient for brickwork	*	Horizontal moment coefficient for blockwork	
0.3	v	0.0136364	v	0.0104444	N/L
0.5	v	0.0242727	v	0.0198889	N/L
0.75	v	0.0326364	v	0.0288889	N/L
1.0	v	0.0386364	v	0.0348889	N/L
1.25	v	0.0426364	v	0.0388889	N/L
1.5	v	0.0456364	v	0.0424444	N/L
1.75	v	0.0476364	v	0.0448889	N/L
	v		v		N/L
	v		v		N/L
	v		v		N/L
	v		v		N/L

all real numbers

RESTRAINT CASE AND CORRESPONDING DATA
Maximum No. (NRE)

RESTRAINT CASE : RESTRAINT CASE H TOP & SIDES FIXED, BASE PINNED

name in characters (maximum number 56)

SHAPE FACTORS AND CORRESPONDING BENDING MOMENT COEFFICIENTS.
MAXIMUM NO. (MAXAPE)

Shape factor	*	* Horizontal moment * coefficient for * brickwork	*	* Horizontal moment * coefficient for * blockwork	
0.3	v	0.0106364	v	0.0084444	N/L
0.5	v	0.0202727	v	0.0158889	N/L
0.75	v	0.0286364	v	0.0244444	N/L
1.0	v	0.0352727	v	0.0308889	N/L
1.25	v	0.0396364	v	0.0354444	N/L
1.5	v	0.0426364	v	0.0388889	N/L
1.75	v	0.0456364	v	0.0418889	N/L
	v		v		N/L
	v		v		N/L
	v		v		N/L
	v		v		N/L

all real numbers

RESTRAINT CASE AND CORRESPONDING DATA
Maximum No. (NRE)

RESTRAINT CASE : | RESTRAINT CASE I ALL SIDES FIXED

              name in characters (maximum number 56)

SHAPE FACTORS AND CORRESPONDING BENDING MOMENT COEFFICIENTS.
MAXIMUM NO. (MAXAPE)

Shape factor	* * *	Horizontal moment coefficient for brickwork	* * *	Horizontal moment coefficient for blockwork	
0.3	v	0.0086364	v	0.0064444	N/L
0.5	v	0.0166364	v	0.0134444	N/L
0.75	v	0.0252727	v	0.0208889	N/L
1.0	v	0.0316364	v	0.0268889	N/L
1.25	v	0.0362727	v	0.0318889	N/L
1.5	v	0.0396364	v	0.0358889	N/L
1.75	v	0.0426364	v	0.0388889	N/L
	v		v		N/L
	v		v		N/L
	v		v		N/L
	v		v		N/L

all real numbers

RESTRAINT CASE AND CORRESPONDING DATA
Maximum No. (NRE)

RESTRAINT CASE : | RESTRAINT CASE J BASE & TOP PINNED, ONE SIDE PINNED |

name in characters (maximum number 56)

SHAPE FACTORS AND CORRESPONDING BENDING MOMENT COEFFICIENTS.
MAXIMUM NO. (MAXAPE)

Shape factor	*	Horizontal moment coefficient for brickwork	*	Horizontal moment coefficient for blockwork	
0.3	v	0.0229091	v	0.0163333	N/L
0.5	v	0.0531818	v	0.0386667	N/L
0.75	v	0.0950909	v	0.0714444	N/L
1.0	v	0.1392727	v	0.1057778	N/L
1.25	v	0.1878182	v	0.1430000	N/L
1.5	v	0.2370909	v	0.1827778	N/L
1.75	v	0.2872727	v	0.2225556	N/L
	v		v		N/L
	v		v		N/L
	v		v		N/L
	v		v		N/L

all real numbers

RESTRAINT CASE AND CORRESPONDING DATA
Maximum No. (NRE)

RESTRAINT CASE : | RESTRAINT CASE K TOP & BASE PINNED, ONE SIDE FIXED |

name in characters (maximum number 56)

SHAPE FACTORS AND CORRESPONDING BENDING MOMENT COEFFICIENTS.
MAXIMUM NO. (MAXAPE)

Shape factor	* * *	Horizontal moment coefficient for brickwork	* * *	Horizontal moment coefficient for blockwork	
0.3	v	0.0202727	v	0.0148889	N/L
0.5	v	0.0435455	v	0.0327778	N/L
0.75	v	0.0728182	v	0.0571111	N/L
1.0	v	0.1014545	v	0.0805556	N/L
1.25	v	0.1260909	v	0.1034444	N/L
1.5	v	0.1490909	v	0.1238889	N/L
1.75	v	0.1697273	v	0.1428889	N/L
	v		v		N/L
	v		v		N/L
	v		v		N/L
	v		v		N/L

all real numbers

RESTRAINT CASE AND CORRESPONDING DATA
Maximum No. (NRE)

RESTRAINT CASE : | RESTRAINT CASE L TOP PINNED, BASE & ONE SIDE FIXED |

                   name in characters (maximum number 56)

SHAPE FACTORS AND CORRESPONDING BENDING MOMENT COEFFICIENTS.
MAXIMUM NO. (MAXAPE)

Shape factor	*	Horizontal moment coefficient for brickwork	*	Horizontal moment coefficient for blockwork	
0.3	v	0.0152727	v	0.0108889	N/L
0.5	v	0.0339091	v	0.0247778	N/L
0.75	v	0.0581818	v	0.0446667	N/L
1.0	v	0.0818182	v	0.0641111	N/L
1.25	v	0.1050909	v	0.0840000	N/L
1.5	v	0.1260909	v	0.1024444	N/L
1.75	v	0.1447273	v	0.1198889	N/L
	v		v		N/L
	v		v		N/L
	v		v		N/L
	v		v		N/L

all real numbers

REFERENCES

1. British Standards Institution, 'Structural Recommendations for Load-bearing Walls', CP.111:1970.

2. British Standards Institution, 'Code of Practice for Structural Use of Masonry', BS.5628:Part 1. Unreinforced masonry : 1978.

3. British Standards Institution, 'The Structural Use of Concrete', CP.110:1972.

4. West, H.W.H., Hodgkinson and Haseltine, B.A. 'The resistance of brickwork to lateral loading', The Structural Engineer, London, Oct. 1977.

5. Haseltine, B.A., West, H.W.H. and Tutt, J.N. 'Design of walls to resist lateral loads', The Structural Engineer, London, Oct. 1977.

6. Timoshenko, S., 'Theory of plates and shells', McGraw-Hill, U.S.A.

7. Johansen, K.W., 'Yield-line formulae for slabs', Cement and Concrete Association, London.

8. British Standards Institution, 'Walling : Brick and Block Masonry', CP.121:Part 1:1973.

9. Haseltine, B.A. and Tutt, J.N., 'External Walls : Design for Wind Loads', Brick Development Association, England, Feb. 1978.

10. British Standards Institution, 'Basic Data for the Design of Buildings', CP.3:Chapter V:Part 2. Wind loads : 1972.

11. Haseltine, B.A. and West, H.W.H., 'A simplified guide to the design of laterally loaded walls', British Ceramic Research Association, Special Publication No. 90.

12. British Standards Institution, 'Clay Bricks and Blocks', BS.3921:1974.

13. Plowman, J.M. and Smith, W.F., 'The selection of damp proof course materials for loadbearing structures', Proceedings S.I.B.M.A.C., April 1970.

14. British Standards Institution, 'Specification for Materials for Damp-Proof Courses', BS.743:1970.

15. Anderson, C. and Bright, N.J., 'Behaviour of non-loadbearing block walls under windloading', Concrete, London, Sept. 1976.

16. British Standards Institution, 'Metal Ties for Cavity Wall Construction', BS.1243:1972.

17. Calderbank, V.J., 'A Course on Programming in Fortran IV', Chapman & Hall, London, 1974.

INDEX